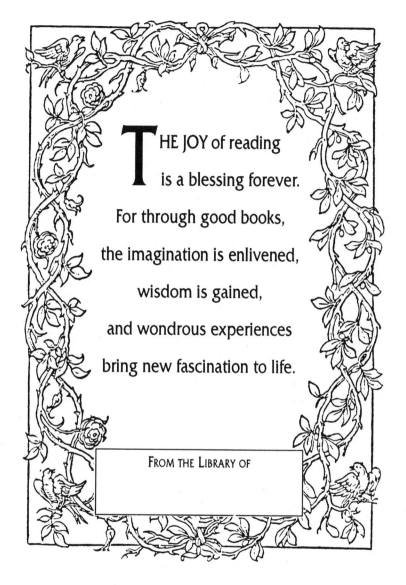

THE JOY of reading
is a blessing forever.
For through good books,
the imagination is enlivened,
wisdom is gained,
and wondrous experiences
bring new fascination to life.

FROM THE LIBRARY OF

LIVING FAITH

LIVING FAITH

Jimmy Carter

TIMES 𝕋 BOOKS

RANDOM HOUSE

Library of Congress Cataloging-in-Publication information is available.

ISBN: 0-8129-2736-2

Book design by Maura Fadden Rosenthal

Manufactured in the United States of America on acid-free paper
9   8   7   6   5   4   3   2

First Edition

*She'd smile, and birds would feel that they no longer
had to sing, or it may be I failed
to hear their song.*

*Within a crowd, I'd hope her glance might be
for me, but knew that she was shy, and wished
to be alone.*

*I'd pay to sit behind her, blind to what
was on the screen, and watch the image flicker
on her hair.*

*I'd glow when her diminished voice would clear
my muddled thoughts, like lightning flashing in
a gloomy sky.*

*The nothing in my soul with her aloof
was changed to foolish fullness when she came
to be with me.*

*With shyness gone and hair caressed with gray,
her smile still makes the birds forget to sing
and me to hear their song.*

Contents

	INTRODUCTION	3
1	THE SEARCH FOR FAITH	16
2	A ROOTED LIFE	39
3	FINDING PEACE AT HOME	61
4	LEADERSHIP AND FAITH	89
5	TO ESTABLISH JUSTICE	107
6	SEARCHING FOR PEACE	135
7	FAITH IN ACTION	161
8	CROSSING BARRIERS	185
9	REACHING OUT	200
10	THE LORD I'VE COME TO KNOW	220
11	ABUNDANT LIFE	236
	ACKNOWLEDGMENTS	257

LIVING FAITH

Introduction

‾‾‾◞◞◞◞◞‾

This is a book about the values and experiences that have shaped my life, and how the religious beliefs I inherited have been transformed into a living faith. I have waited a long time to write these words, because religion is a private matter—and my own faith has been the subject of much public speculation. Yet I think that my close relationship with God is something I share with many Americans of different traditions.

I hope this book will be illuminating for those who have wondered whether a "born-again Christian" president was a contradiction in terms, or why a candidate for the highest office in the land who was far ahead in the polls gave a particular interview to *Playboy* magazine and almost lost the election.

I've had a varied life and a dramatic one, with times of wonderful accomplishment alongside devastating setbacks. Some of my career changes were of my own choosing, and others have been forced on me by what I considered at the time to be failures. I have moved from a naval career to farming, to business, then to a political life, and, since the end of my presidency, to a challenging and delightful life as a college professor, a volunteer activist, and a grandfather. I have been blessed with a loving and enduring marriage and have attained many of the goals I set for myself as a young man. But I have also witnessed the deaths of my father and siblings when they were far too young, confronted public defeat more times than I wanted, and faced bankruptcy as well as the self-doubt, private losses, and disappointments that are part of the human lot.

Throughout these three score and ten years, my faith as a Christian has provided the necessary stability in my life. Come to think of it, stability is not exactly the right word, because to have faith in something is an inducement not to dormancy but to action. To me, *faith* is not just a noun but also a verb.

Faith is the foundation of this book, and it is a rich, complex, even elusive concept, used in varied ways in the Scriptures. In Christian tradition, the concept of faith has two interrelated meanings, both implying fidelity: confidence in a being (God), and action based on firm belief.

The clearest New Testament definition is "Faith is the

assurance of things hoped for, the conviction of things not seen" (Hebrews 11:1). The text continues, "By faith we understand that the universe was formed at God's command, so that what is seen was not made out of what was visible" (Heb. 11:3). The Bible goes on to say that we are justified, sanctified, and reconciled with God by faith, not by works or by obeying the law; the just shall live by faith; God gave each of us a measure of faith; we walk by faith, not sight; we are children of God by faith; we are saved by grace through faith; faith is the gift of God, and it is more precious than gold; to face life, we should put on the shield of faith, the breastplate of faith and love; we are taught in faith and truth.

In this book, I explore some of the ways my Christian faith has guided and sustained me, as well as the ways it has challenged and driven me to seek a closer relationship with God and my fellow human beings.

These chapters began as an outgrowth of the Bible classes I have been teaching ever since I became an adult. When I was a young midshipman at the U.S. Naval Academy, I taught the children of the officers and enlisted men stationed at Annapolis. Later, while serving on submarines, I conducted religious services on special days, such as Easter. A dozen or more of the crew would sit on folding bunks between the torpedoes, and I would stand alongside the launching tubes to read the text, ask and answer some questions if I could, and say a prayer. After I left the navy and returned home to Plains,

Georgia, I taught young boys and girls in Sunday school regularly for about fifteen years, as my father had always done when I was a child. Even as president, while I was attending Washington's First Baptist Church, the regular teacher and I would set aside a few Sundays each year for me to teach the adult class.

Today, in Plains, I lead an adult class at Maranatha Baptist Church, a congregation of about forty-five families, most of whom have lived and worshiped together for several generations. ("Maranatha," meaning "Come, Lord," is the first Christian prayer of which we have any record [1 Corinthians 16:22].) Since most of our adult members are teaching their own classes, keeping the nursery, or managing other Sunday school affairs, almost all my students are visitors. They are families who drive over from nearby towns, entire Bible classes from more distant communities who come in buses to worship with us, or vacationers who stop by on journeys to or from Florida. Quite often, one or two will whisper to me that they have never been in a church before, or not since they were baptized as babies.

Along with the visitors who join us from nearby towns or distant communities are two special groups. One is from a nearby community known as Koinonia Partners (*koinonia* is a Greek word meaning "brotherhood"). This farm was organized in the early 1940s by Dr. Clarence Jordan, who designed it to break down the strict racial barriers that existed in the South during those days. A few dedicated and courageous white Christians invited poor black families to live, work, and worship with them on an equal basis. For years they survived economic boycotts by almost all the local merchants and attacks by the Ku Klux Klan and other white segregationist groups, who burned their property and fired bullets through their homes at night. For more than fifty years, they have lived on the proceeds of their farming and with the help of supporters throughout the country.

The other regular members and frequent visitors in my class come from the international headquarters of Habitat for Humanity, which originated at Koinonia about twenty years ago. Habitat is described more fully later in this book; it is a worldwide program of building homes for "God's people in need." Both the temporary volunteers and permanent workers at Koinonia and Habitat attempt to demonstrate their own religious faith by serving the poor and needy in an often sacrificial way.

Most of the time it is a pleasure for me to study the suggested Scripture, consider at least overnight how best to present the lesson, read some commentaries, prepare an outline, and then meet with my class on Sunday mornings. I treat theological arguments gingerly but am bolder when it comes to connecting my religious beliefs with life and current events in the world, even when the issues are controversial.

I learned long ago that the best way to finesse a difficult Bible passage is to involve the class in a give-and-take discussion. Questions back and forth keep us all awake and help us understand the subject. We have lively debates but few injured feelings. Some of the exchanges continue after the services are over, even in letters that come to me during the following weeks.

I have discovered during these years of teaching that it is far better not to preach and just share the lesson on an equal basis with those who have come to join me. The more memorable experiences are when we meld into a common group, all striving to decipher the meaning of the Bible verses and to apply the message to our own lives. My hope is similarly to maintain an equal or shared relationship with the readers of this book, so that we can search together for religious truths, how they relate to us, and perhaps how they can affect our lives.

These classes often include representatives from a dozen Protestant denominations, including Mennonites and Amish, as well as Jews and Catholics. One recent Sunday, I had visitors from twenty-eight foreign countries. We all have a feeling of being part of a community of people trying together to make sense of our lives and of our world. Because of this diversity, I've had to go more deeply into other people's questions—some of which I have never raised in my own life.

And so I began writing this book by trying to use the most meaningful of these classes as a base for thinking about a "living faith." However, as the months went by and I wondered aloud with my family and friends, I realized that the story was more complicated than biblical texts and their relationship to my life. I saw that the debate about faith in American life has, if anything, intensified since I was president.

As a new millennium approaches, we Americans face many issues within which religion, politics, and private matters tend to mix explosively. They create sharp divisions among us, in our private and public lives and even in individual religious denominations. It seems increasingly difficult to separate church and state issues, and even the purely religious issues have to be addressed by politicians.

I have confronted the separation of church and state from both directions. I think often of the strong reaction of our visiting revival preacher when I decided to run for my first political office back in 1962. He asked me, "How can you, as a Christian, a deacon, and a Sunday school teacher, become involved in politics?" I gave him a smart-aleck response: "I will have 75,000 people in my senate district. How would you like to have a congregation that big?"

More recently, since our White House years, my move has been away from politics and toward religion, but for me the two are still related. There is no doubt that my having been a national political leader is what attracts most visitors to my Sunday school class, and it is clear to me that these worshipers are increasingly eager to help shape our nation's political agenda.

When I look back on my life, I can see how startling the changes have been. Eric Hoffer, the self-educated longshoreman and philosopher, described the 1930s as a time of hope and more recent years as a time of desire. As a child, I knew the '30s to be a time of hope, when the economic situation was so bad that everyone believed it could only improve. Nowadays, things are so plentiful, at least as shown in movies and on television, that we want not only what we already have but also what everyone else has.

I was brought up in a fairly isolated rural community called Archery, about three miles west of Plains, and in a family that was close and cohesive. Home was our haven, in times of pain or pleasure. There was no doubt that my father made the final decisions, but all of us knew that Mama's influence and opinions were always major factors in how our family was managed. There were certain aspects of life, particularly in the running of the household and the raising of my sisters, that were almost exclusively my mother's purview. Together, our parents were dominant, and we children respected and obeyed them. In fact, I never deliberately disobeyed them.

Now most Americans move around frequently and are exposed to many influences, and our environments and customs are multifaceted. But for me as a child, there were just a few sources of knowledge about myself or any other people. Our contacts with the world beyond our community were limited. Without electricity in our house, time on the battery radio was restricted, even on the rare nights when we stayed up after dark. We did listen as a family to *Little Orphan Annie*, *Fibber McGee and Molly*, and *Amos 'n' Andy*, and my parents would sometimes let me stay up until 8:00 P.M. to hear Glenn Miller's band playing the current musical hits. But that was all the outside world I knew.

In addition to my family and our farm neighbors, almost all African-American, I knew other people just through school and the church. Our prom parties, which parents would carefully orchestrate to let boys and girls get acquainted, were sponsored by the church.

Sunday mornings were for Sunday school and preaching at Plains Baptist Church, where Daddy was a teacher and a deacon. After church we always had the best meal of the week, usually fried chicken, mashed potatoes, hot biscuits, and all kinds of vegetables, followed by pies made from sweet potatoes or fruits of the season. Afterward, our activities were severely limited. There were no stores open, movies in the nearby county seat were out of the question, and shooting a gun or playing cards was prohibited. Fishing in the nearby creek or small pond was a close call, but it came to be permitted if done discreetly. It would not have been appropriate to walk down a public road with a fishing pole.

My mama and daddy played cards—but certainly not on Sunday. Rosalynn points out that others, including her own family, wouldn't play cards at all.

At the age of twelve, when I was deemed old enough to drive a car by myself, my sisters and I went back to the church on Sunday evenings for meetings of the Baptist Young People's Union, or BYPU. (Our brother Billy was thirteen years younger than I.) This was very important, because the BYPU sponsored most of the teenage social events.

I need not go on, since the picture is fairly clear. It was a simple, family-centered, deeply religious, working existence, with easy interracial play with my black neighbors.

I imagine that, except for automobiles and a hand-cranked telephone, our lives were similar to those of our great-grandparents.

There was a special closeness among neighbors. Sickness or death were community affairs. Even in later years, when my father was on his deathbed, the yard was full of people who came to offer cakes, pies, and fried chicken so that we wouldn't have to do anything but care for him. Daddy had cancer, and everyone knew that his illness was terminal. He grew weaker every day because he couldn't eat or digest any food, but folks would go out, even if it wasn't quail season, kill a couple, and bring the carefully cooked birds to my daddy with some pecan pie or something they knew he really liked. There was a sharing not just of food but of presence.

Now, of course, family life even in the small Plains community is quite different. Some activities once strictly concealed in our proper society are probably no more prevalent but are now out in the open. Divorce has become acceptable, even for active church members. Without trying to analyze it too deeply, I see that one of the most significant changes is the relationship between young people and their parents. The ties are substantially broken during the teen years, no matter how much parents want to retain strong influence over their growing children. The outside world is a much more powerful influence, with the availability of rapid transportation, television, and particularly a broader circle of friends (and adversaries), whose influence often exceeds that of our own families.

But many families still have a core of principles that do not change. Where do we turn now when there is a moral question? What things in the 1990s are the same as they were in the 1930s? We need a permanent foundation on which our lives can be fashioned. Without a central core of beliefs or standards by which to live, we may never experience the challenge and excitement of seeking a greater life. We will have ceased to grow, like Jesus, "strong in spirit, filled with wisdom; and the grace of God upon him" (Luke 2:40).

People in the New Testament church came to Paul and asked him what things they could depend on if they changed their way of living and adopted the Christian faith that he espoused. He replied, "We look not at what can be seen but at what cannot be seen; for what can be seen is temporary, but what cannot be seen is eternal" (2 Corinthians 4:18). The things we cannot see are paramount, and do not change—those about which Jesus taught. Can we see truth, justice, forgiveness, or love? I try to remember this verse during some of the more trying times of my own life, and I use it frequently in my classes and in counseling people who are distressed about crises in their lives.

It is not difficult to identify the changes in our lives, some welcome and others quite painful. But we don't want

the verities of our lives to change. We need to have something unshakable, like a mother's love, something that can't
be destroyed by war, the loss of a loved one, lack of success
in business, a serious illness, or failure to realize our ambitions. We need some foundation on which we can build a
predictable and dependable existence.

This cannot be found in either our nation's laws or religious denominations. I would like to say as an American
who has been president of the United States that the
accepted values of my country are constant—but they
aren't. There's a great deal of change, all the time, in the
interpretation of laws and in the passage of new ones. Some
laws violate what seem to be accepted principles and create
serious division within our society. Also, almost every
religious denomination is fragmenting over controversial
secular issues.

But despite the confusion and controversy among religious organizations, there are basic principles that, for me,
have never changed. For a Christian, the life and teachings
of Jesus offer a sound moral foundation that includes all the
most basic elements that should guide us. Since these
highest standards are eternal, we have an obligation to
comprehend what they are and what they mean for us. Our
faith can provide enough courage to apply these biblical
lessons to our daily lives. If specific guidelines or examples
are not always available, at least our basic principles can
help narrow the options.

For me, sharing any problem through prayer provides a
powerful element of calm and objectivity. Then, when I
might fear or regret the consequences of a choice I have

made, an awareness of the presence of the Spirit of God can give me courage. John says that Christ knows us all (John 2:24), and Paul reminds us that nothing can separate us from the love of God (Romans 8:39). Somewhat to my own surprise, this has become a book whose core is love—the love that is possible among those who are closely related, among strangers allied by a common dream or faith, and even between people who begin by despising each other but find a way to see the image of God in each other's humanity.

When I return to my beginnings, I see a number of times when what I believed I wanted most was challenged by a more difficult path. When I had the courage to choose that path, even in the midst of despair and uncertainty, I was given a glimpse of deeper truths that continue to sustain me.

The Search for Faith

Religious faith has always been at the core of my existence. It has been a changing and evolving experience, beginning when I was a child of three, memorizing Bible verses in Sunday school. When I was nine years old, I was promoted to the Sunday school class taught by my father, so I had the double influence of the church environment and my own father as my teacher. My faith at first was simple and unequivocal; there was no doubt in my mind about the truth of what I learned in church.

Yet even as a child, I was dismayed to find myself becoming skeptical about some aspects of my inherited faith. We learned in church that Jesus had risen from the dead three days after his crucifixion, and that all believers would someday enjoy a similar resurrection. As I grew older, I began to wonder whether this could be so. I became quite concerned about it, worried not so much about the prospect of my own death as about the possibility that I might be separated from my mother and father. These two people were the core of my existence, and I couldn't bear the idea that I wouldn't be with them forever.

By the time I was twelve or thirteen years old, my anxiety about this became so intense that at the end of every prayer, until after I was an adult, before "Amen" I added the words "And, God, please help me believe in the resurrection." What made it worse was that I thought I was the only person with such concerns. I felt guilty that I doubted what the preacher said and what my father taught me in Sunday school.

This was not the kind of thing we would have talked about at home. Although my father was at ease teaching the lessons in church, I think he would have been embarrassed to bring up Christian subjects with me while we were at work in the fields or sitting together at the dinner table. In a way, I saw a different father in Sunday school. I admired Daddy greatly as a man who excelled in many things: he was an unbeatable tennis player, an outstanding baseball pitcher, and a fine hunter and fisherman; he knew how to raise bird dogs so they could find and point quail, and he was a successful farmer and businessman. I took his faith and his Sunday school teaching for granted, and I kept my doubts to myself. It would have been inconceivable to express doubts to him about anything in the Bible.

So even at an early age, I was developing a kind of dual approach to biblical teachings. My sense of faith was preeminent: I *knew* that there was a God who was our creator and that I was being observed and judged in all I did; I *knew* that Jesus Christ had accepted the punishment for my sins and that through faith in him I could be saved. But I had a nagging degree of skepticism about the relationship between my faith and the scientific point of view I was already developing through my schoolwork and my reading.

Of course, church was much more to me than a source of knowledge about God. It was the center of social life for our family and for the whole community. For example, we had no Boy Scout troop in Plains then, so my father would take his Sunday school class into the woods to camp out all night or go fishing, teaching the town boys something about the outdoors.

Beginning when I was ten or twelve, church was also the place where we became acquainted with our female classmates in a social setting. The church would sponsor closely chaperoned "prom parties" for the young people on Friday nights. Each of us would bring a pound of food—a pound of fried chicken, pork barbecue, bread, potato salad, or cake. Then we'd stroll, talk, and dance. The chaperones made sure there were no wallflowers at these parties, and we had to check back in with them frequently enough to minimize opportunities for "improper" conduct. Prom cards were used to keep track of partners for dances, and no one could dance more than three times, or spend more than fifteen consecutive minutes, with the same partner.

These parties were fun, and as I grew older I came to realize that they were also the way our parents arranged for us to explore the field for possible future spouses. Every summer, our Baptist church held a revival week, designed to heighten the religious commitment of the church members and to convince nonmembers to join. (The Methodist church held its own revival at a different time of year, and the more devout Christians in town would attend both.) The visiting preachers who conducted the ten revival services offered a two-part message. They preached what we called "hellfire and damnation" sermons to convince us that anyone who didn't accept Christ as a personal savior was going to hell. Interspersed was a description of the glorious alternative of redemption and heaven offered by Jesus. Their eloquence and the power of their message were often overwhelming.

Practically everyone in Plains would come to some of these services. There was a morning sermon at ten o'clock, attended by the women while their children were in school and their husbands worked in the stores and fields, and a nighttime service, which entire families could attend. The climax of each sermon was when nonmembers were asked to come forward and declare their intention of accepting Christ as savior. This was the most important step in life, marking the moment at which a person became a member of the Christian community. It was much more important for us Baptists than the rite of baptism, which came soon afterward and symbolized a burial of our old selves with immersion, rebirth into a new life with Christ, and membership in our church.

We didn't believe in what we called "child conversions," although I understand that in some Baptist churches children as young as eight might make the step of accepting Christ and becoming church members. We were encouraged to wait until we were older, and I decided to accept Christ during a revival service when I was eleven. I was then baptized with other new converts on the Sunday following revival week.

What does it mean when I say that I "decided to accept Christ"? Jesus was the Messiah, the long-awaited savior, who came both to reveal God to us and to heal the division between God and humankind. As Jesus told his disciples, "If you have seen me, you have seen God" (John 14:9). Furthermore, the Gospels recount how Jesus, having lived a perfect and blameless life, accepted a death of horrible suffering on the cross on our behalf, as an atonement for the sins we have committed. Accepting Christ as my savior means believing all these things and entering into a relationship with God through him, so that my past and future sins no longer alienate me from my Creator.

Putting our total faith in these concepts is what is meant by being "born again." It's when there is an intimate melding of my life with that of Jesus: I become a brother with him, and God is our mutual parent. This frees me from the strings that previously limited my relationship with my creator.

Being born again is a new life, not of perfection but of striving, stretching, and searching—a life of intimacy with God through the Holy Spirit. There must first be an emptying, and then a refilling. To the extent that we want to

know, understand, and experience God, we ca⸍
in Jesus. It is a highly personal and subjectiv⸍
possible only if we are searching for greater ∪ ∪⸍
ourselves and God.

This experience is challenging, even painful at times, but ultimately deeply rewarding. It provides answers to the most disturbing questions about our existence, the purpose of life, and how to deal with sorrow, failure, loneliness, guilt, and fear. In it, we come to know that our gifts from God are not earned by our own acts but are given to us through his grace. As Paul says, "Therefore, since we have been justified through faith, we have peace with God through our Lord Jesus Christ, through whom we have gained access by faith into this grace in which we now stand" (Romans 5:1–2).

The love of Christ lets us feel the fullness of God. Ephesians 3:16–19 describes this experience well:

> I pray that, according to the riches of his glory, he may grant
> that you may be strengthened in your inner being with power
> through his Spirit, and that Christ may dwell in your hearts
> through faith, as you are being rooted and grounded in love.
> I pray that you may have the power to comprehend, with all
> the saints, what is the breadth and length and height and
> depth, and to know the love of Christ that surpasses knowl-
> edge, so that you may be filled with all the fullness of God.

Being born again didn't happen to me when I was eleven. For me, it has been an evolutionary thing. Rather than a flash of light or a sudden vision of God speaking, it involved a series of steps that have brought me steadily closer to Christ. My conversion at eleven was just one of these steps.

Through it all, my worry over the doubts I felt about some Christian teachings continued, and my skepticism was somewhat heightened when I went away to college. I took part in the usual all-night discussions with my freshman and sophomore classmates about big philosophical topics: Why was I created? What is the purpose of life? Who or what is God? We questioned everything, and we thought we were quite profound.

Then I went to the U.S. Naval Academy, and I became an engineer and later studied advanced science. This was also the first time that I got to know significant numbers of people who were not Protestant Christians. (There were a handful of Jews in our nearby county seat of Americus—respected community members—but their religion was never discussed.) At the Naval Academy, there were many students who attended Protestant religious services, a substantial number who attended Roman Catholic services, and a relatively small number who attended Jewish services. (We also had a few who claimed to be Moslems, Hindus, or atheists, but the rest of us all figured that this was so they wouldn't have to go to the mandatory chapel services.) So for the first time, I had the opportunity to learn something about other faiths.

Worshiping God remained an important part of my life. During my three years at the academy, I attended chapel regularly, and I got to know the chaplain pretty well. I also taught Sunday school; my students were the nine-to-twelve-year-old daughters of the enlisted men and officers who were assigned permanently to the naval base at Annapolis. Out of 3,500 midshipmen, only a handful were equally active in chapel activities, so this was a significant religious commitment on my part.

When I graduated from Annapolis, Rosalynn and I were married, and she moved from the Methodist church in which she'd grown up to join me as a Baptist. However, the following seven years I spent in the navy were a relatively dormant phase in my religious life. With me assigned to various ships at naval bases in Virginia, Hawaii, California, and Connecticut, it wasn't convenient for Rosalynn and me to be part of a single nurturing church community.

Nonetheless, I sought out opportunities to worship when and where I could. For instance, when I got off duty on Sunday mornings after several days at sea, I would almost invariably find a Christian church service to attend on the naval base, despite the fact that I was eager to get home to my young bride. It didn't matter to me what kind of service I went to—I attended either Protestant or Roman Catholic services, and took communion at the Catholic masses; I just went to whichever service was earliest, so I could get home sooner.

Seven years after Annapolis, I was enjoying a burgeoning navy career when I was called home to my father's deathbed. This proved to be a turning point in my spiritual life.

During the weeks before and after my father's death, my

family's immersion in the Christian community of Plains was an overwhelming experience for me. I felt that we had a family with not five people in it but several hundred. This was something I had almost forgotten since I'd left home as a teenager. My appreciation for the warmth and power of this Christian fellowship was a major factor in my decision to leave the navy and return to live in Plains.

As soon as we'd moved home, I volunteered to teach Sunday school at the Plains Baptist Church again, taking over my father's own class (the juniors, aged nine to twelve). After a year, Rosalynn joined me as a teacher of the junior girls, while I taught the boys. Soon I became head of the junior department, and also a deacon, one of the important lay ministries in the Baptist church.

My religious questions persisted, however, made more intense, in a way, by my father's death. This was the first real tragedy in my life. (I had lost my grandparents earlier, but they had lived in another community and I was not very close to them.) I found my father's death hard to understand. How could a good man, not nearly as old as many others in Plains, be deprived by God of his productive life? It seemed to me a harsh act, one I could only attribute to what I thought of as the God of the Old Testament, a stern, judgmental figure, very different from the loving, forgiving Jesus I knew from the Gospels.

This is when I began to explore in some depth the writings of theologians. I had never taken a course in religion or theology, but now I bought a large number of books by

authors like Dietrich Bonhoeffer, Karl Barth, Martin
Buber, Paul Tillich, Hans Küng, and particularly Reinhold
Niebuhr, and I began to read and examine their ideas.
I explored more deeply what religion is, considering
how my scientific outlook and knowledge, my continuing
doubts about the biblical accounts of miracles, and my un-
easiness about the relationship between God the Creator
and God in Christ could be accommodated to the traditional faith I'd inherited. A torturous time of searching followed. I struggled to understand and differentiate the
varying definitions of religion and the nature of God that I
found in the works of theologians and philosophers, looking for a point of view with which I could feel comfortable.

I was fascinated by the outlooks of these thinkers, but
my own relationship to faith remained an open question.
An important part of the answer came to me from the writings of Paul Tillich. One of his themes is that doubt is an
acceptable, even necessary aspect of faith—that faith im-
plies a continuing search, not necessarily a final answer.

I found myself turning repeatedly to the story in the
Gospel of Mark when a father comes to Jesus in search of
a cure for his son, who is suffering seizures. The father asks
Jesus to heal his son, saying, "If you can do anything, have
pity on us and help us." Jesus replies, "If you can believe!
All things are possible to him who believes." And the father
responds, "I believe; help my unbelief!" Jesus rebukes the
spirit and drives it away from the son, healing him completely (Mark 9:17–27).

The assurance Jesus offers in this story—that we will
not be turned away on account of our doubts or skepticism

but that he will "help our unbelief"—has meant a great deal to me, especially in times of pain or trouble. At such times, I've felt strongly the need of something more permanent and profound than a successful career, being president, or even my relationship with Rosalynn. Jesus' acceptance has given me this.

Maybe some Christians never lack faith—they are the lucky ones. However, I don't know of anybody who has never had doubts about any aspect of the Christian faith.

We would like to have an absolutely certain base on which to build our lives—unquestioned faith in everything that the Bible tells us about God, about Jesus, about a quality life, about life after death, about God's love for us. Perhaps we are afraid that opening the door to a little questioning might shake the foundation of our faith or anger God. But I came to realize that it is a mistake not to face our doubts courageously. We should be willing to ask questions, always searching for a closer relationship with God, a more profound faith in Christ. It is foolish to think that our own doubts can change the truth.

When I contemplated abandoning my naval career, I prayed fervently that God would guide me to the right decision. Later, when I lost the 1966 governor's election and was tempted to abandon my faith altogether, my search for God's will sustained me through my anger and disillusionment. I have seen many people with broken lives, some on the verge of alcoholism or even suicide, turn and construct new and vibrant lives based on religious faith. The combined testimonies of countless people with similar experiences have helped to perpetuate religious faith as an integral part of the lives of billions of believers.

Yet the acquiring of faith is not an easy or frivolous thing. How can we prove that God created the universe, that the prophets communicated with God, that Jesus was the Messiah, or that the resurrection occurred? How can we prove that our lives are meaningful, that truth exists, or that we love or are loved? When I become absorbed in these questions, it helps me to fall back on my faith as a Christian.

The Danish existentialist Søren Kierkegaard said, "Faith means the betting of one's life upon the God in Jesus Christ, . . . the giving or commitment of one's whole life." My faith—my life commitment—has been instilled in me since childhood. Despite periods of doubt, it has been confirmed and strengthened by the tangible spiritual benefits I have received from the "assurance of things hoped for, the conviction of things not seen" (Hebrews 11:1). It is only through faith that I can maintain a relationship with the omnipotent Creator and my personal savior. Without this, I would feel destitute.

My reading of theology, which helped to open these new ideas about faith for me, was an illuminating experience in which I began to feel at ease with my religion for the first time since I was a little child.

I also began to see that my Christian faith and my scientific outlook could be compatible, not conflicting. One of the Bible passages that has helped me understand this is found in Paul's letter to the Romans. Speaking about the pagan peoples of the day, Paul wrote, "That which is known about God is evident within them, for God made it evident to them. For since the creation of the world His invisible attributes, His eternal power and divine nature, have been clearly seen, being understood through what has been made, so that they are without excuse" (Romans 1:19–20). Paul's point was that the glories of the world around us prove God's existence.

Like Paul, I see the glory of God around me, in the unfathomable mysteries of the universe and the diversity and intricacies of creation. We stand in wonder at how a tree grows from an acorn, how a flower blooms, or how DNA can shape the appearance and character of a living creature. It is almost humanly incomprehensible that in our Milky Way galaxy there are billions of stars equivalent to our sun, and then billions of other galaxies equivalent to our own. At the other end of the scale, I marvel that the inseparable atom I learned about in high school is really a collection of remarkable components, matter and anti-matter, rotating in different directions yet held together by forces of immense power, and some particles able to pass through the entire earth without being deflected.

Even more miraculous is the human form, in which the trillions of neuron connections in a single human brain exceed the total number of celestial bodies in the known heavens! Scientific knowledge only enhances my sense of God's glory filling the universe. Over the centuries, scientists have discovered more and more about these truths— truths that have always existed. None of these discoveries contradicts my belief in an ultimate and superior being; they simply confirm the reverence and awe generated by what becomes known and what remains unexplained. As a believer, I have no problem with discoveries in astronomy, geology, and paleontology: that the universe is enormous and expanding, the earth is ancient, and human beings have evolved from primitive ancestors. It is not difficult for me to accept the "big bang" theory of the origin of the universe, at least until it is refuted by further exploration of the heavens and a new explanation is evolved to explain what God has done. Nor does it shake my religious faith to realize that the early authors of the Scriptures thought that the earth was flat, that stars were little things like Christmas tree ornaments that could fall on us, that the entire process of creation occurred during six earthly days, and that the first woman came from the rib of the first man, both Adam and Eve created in modern human form. The gap between their understanding and ours just indicates that knowledge was revealed later to Galileo, Newton, Darwin, Einstein, and Hubble—and to most of us.

One of my favorite authors is Stephen Jay Gould, an evolutionary biologist who writes monthly articles for *Natural History* magazine, which are later published in book form. His most intriguing book for me was *Wonderful Life*, in which he described the remarkable creatures that evolved almost overnight (in geological terms) during the Cambrian period, about 530 million years ago. He claimed that if a few genes or some environmental factors had been different, the "tape of life" as we know it would have played out in a completely different way. Everything has been a matter of chance or accident, including the evolution of human beings.

Feeling a bit presumptuous, I wrote to Gould disagreeing with this premise and asserting that there were factors other than pure happenstance that influenced the course of evolution. He later contradicted my argument—with good humor—in another of his books, *Bully for Brontosaurus*. Such discussions will continue on many fronts, as more scientific discoveries are made. The fact is that between true scientific facts and faith in a supreme being, the Creator of all, there can be no disparity—except among people who argue about things that cannot be or have not yet been proven.

Later, I wrote a poem on the subject:

A CONTEMPLATION OF WHAT HAS BEEN CREATED, AND WHY

I tried to fathom nature's laws
from twirling models and schoolroom sketches
of molecules and parts of atoms,
and nearly believed—but then came quarks,
bosons, leptons, antiparticles,
opposite-turning mirror images,
some that perforate the earth,
never swerving from their certain paths.
I've listened to conflicting views
about the grand and lesser worlds:
a big bang where it all began;

of curved, ever-expanding space;
perhaps tremendous whirling yo-yos
that will someday reach the end
of cosmic gravity and then
fly back to where they can restart
or cataclysmically blow apart—
and then, and then the next event.
And will it be an accident?

Unlike Professor Gould, I am sure that none of this is an accident. If Paul expected the ancient Romans to believe in God because of their relatively limited observations of the world around them, shouldn't our faith be stronger, since we know so much more?

In its own way, technology offers a lesson in the nature of faith. Aren't there plenty of things in modern life that we believe but can't understand? The computer, radio, television, space travel—all once seemed miraculous, but most of us now accept them as routine. We can set up an antenna and bring in 150 different television programs. The waves are all around us, plus countless radio signals, waiting for us to extract them from the ether for our pleasure or information. There is no way for us to detect in advance that the signals are here, or for most of us to explain how these electromagnetic waves can be changed into music or colored, moving pictures almost instantaneously. These are amazing things that few of us comprehend, but we believe them.

In the same way, I cannot fully understand many reli-

gious concepts, even some aspects of the life of Christ—the
extremes of love and judgment, power and weakness, the
demand for perfection and total forgiveness, the omnipo-
tence of God and his human Son weeping and tempted.
The totality of it is overwhelming, but I accept it with confidence—through faith.

In addition to the intellectual realization of a supreme
being, we have a purely subjective need to meet a personal
yearning. We have an innate desire to relate to the all-
knowing, the all-powerful, and the ever-present—to some
entity that transcends ourselves. I am grateful and happy
when I feel the presence of God within me, as a tangible
influence on my thoughts and on the ultimate standards of
my life. It is reassuring to me to know that God will always
be with me and cares for me. I think of the words of Isaiah:
"When you pass through the waters, I will be with you; and
through the rivers, they shall not overwhelm you; when
you walk through fire you shall not be burned, and the
flame shall not consume you. For I am the Lord your
God. . . . You are precious in my sight, and honored, and I
love you" (Isaiah 43:2–4).

Our Sunday school class often becomes involved in a
discussion about how to achieve this closeness to God.
Except in moments of crisis, when we reach desperately for
some sustaining force, the relationship requires some
effort on our part, some reaching out. I remind my class of
the man in terrible trouble who prayed, "God, if you'll just
get me out of this mess, I promise never to bother you with

my prayers again." We need God's presence at all times—
not just when life is at its most difficult.

This desire for a personal relationship with God cannot
be abolished, even under pressure. A basic reason for the
disintegration of the once-powerful Soviet Union is that
the government required its citizens to put all their faith
in the central authority. The communist apparatus—
including the army, the party, and the government—was
declared to be sufficient to meet all human needs. As Karl
Marx said, religion was considered merely "the opium of
the people." Eventually, this entire system collapsed, a
hollow shell. Eighty years after the Soviet government officially declared atheism dominant and prohibited religion,
the seeds of faith still exist, and there is now an explosion
of religious fervor in Russia.

There are other elements in our lives that make us turn
to Christ, to seek God's will, to excel in our own standards
of morality or belief. We want to prove that our lives are
meaningful. At the same time, faith has to be predicated on
a *desire* to believe. The Leonard Cohen song about Christ's
walking on the water says that Jesus knew that "only
drowning men could see him." Faced with death, in a
storm, the disciples wanted to believe.

I've been disconcerted to find my own religious beliefs
incompatible with those of many prominent Baptists. In
1976, during my first campaign for the presidency, I was
taken aback when the evangelist Jerry Falwell condemned
me because I "claimed" to be a Christian. At the time, I dis-

counted the importance of this criticism, especially since
few people then knew who Jerry Falwell was, but before
the end of my term in office, he and his organization, the
Moral Majority, became quite famous. This was the first
national emergence of the so-called Christian Right, later
joined by Pat Robertson, the Christian Coalition, and
others.

In 1979, this conservative wing of Christianity was
strong enough to take over leadership of the Southern
Baptist Convention (SBC), which had always been my
church "home." I was a longtime, stalwart supporter of the
SBC, which represented Baptist congregations totaling 14
million members. I'd served on the fifteen-man board of
the Convention's Brotherhood Commission, which sets
policy for all the men's affairs and programs, and had even
conducted the wedding ceremony for the commission's
executive director while I was governor of Georgia (the
only wedding I've ever performed). So I was dismayed
when the fundamentalists took control of the convention's
organization and began purging the more moderate
leaders and defining narrowly the criteria for seminary
professors and curricula.

In the United States today, there seems to be a growing
split between two ways of practicing the Christian faith.
On the one hand, there are those who believe that Christianity gives its adherents material benefits. Such churches
promise their members comfort, security, financial wealth,
and prestige, and they often display an evangelistic zeal
that is quite impressive. Many of these churches are very
active in public affairs and have become powerful political

forces. On the other hand, there are those who consider ministering to the poor, the despised, and the homeless as important elements of Christianity. The first group often looks upon the second as less than truly Christian, sometimes using the phrase "secular humanist" to describe them.

I have been faced with this charge. A high official of the Southern Baptist Convention came into the Oval Office to visit me when I was president. As he and his wife were leaving, he said, "We are praying, Mr. President, that you will abandon secular humanism as your religion." This was a shock to me. I didn't know what he meant, and I am still not sure. He may have said this because I was against a constitutional amendment to authorize mandatory prayer in public schools and had been working on some things opposed by the "religious right," such as the Panama Canal treaties, a Department of Education, and the SALT II treaty with the Soviets.

These differences among Christian groups sap a tremendous portion of our ability, time, money, and influence. Much of our energy is spent in internecine warfare, in arguments and debates that not only are divisive but incapacitate us for our work in the name of Christ.

Our faith should be a guide for us in deciding between the permanent and the transient, the important and the insignificant, the gratifying and the troubling, the joyful and the depressing. We must study the principles on which our faith is founded, but we can't become obsessed with the belief that we have a special ordination from God to interpret the Scriptures and to consider anyone who disagrees with us wrong and inferior. The tendency of fundamentalists, in Christianity and other religions, to condemn those who differ from them is perhaps the most disturbing aspect of their current ascendancy.

Of course, the fellowship of faith is even larger than the Christian world. The first great Christian theologian, Paul, repeatedly emphasized the fundamental importance of faith as a unifying force between Christians and Jews. A burning question in the early church was whether God's covenant with Abraham was exclusively for the Jews. Some feared that if they became Christians they would forgo God's blessing. Paul made it clear that it was the patriarch's faith and not his ethnicity that was significant. He relied on the Scripture: "For the promise that he should be the heir of the world was not to Abraham or to his seed, through the law, but through the righteousness of faith" (Romans 4:13). The covenant with God is shared by Jews and Christians, with faith in one God as the unifying element.

Although the word *faith* is used only twice in the King James Version of the Old Testament (245 times in the New Testament), the writer of Hebrews relates faith directly and by name to a large number of biblical heroes of earlier times whose actions were determined by it. Through faith, Noah built his ark and became the heir of righteousness. Abraham and his wife, Sarah, although "as good as dead," had descendants as numerous as the stars because of their faith. Joseph, near death, had faith enough to call for the exodus of the Israelites from Egypt. Moses gave up the "pleasures of sin" to lead the Jews to freedom, depending on his faith to sustain him through forty years in the wilderness. And through faith, Gideon, Samson, David, Samuel, and the prophets conquered kingdoms, administered justice, shut the mouths of lions, quenched flames, escaped the edges of swords, and had weaknesses turned to strengths. The power of faith is a unifying bond between Christian and Jew and between the heroes of ancient Israel and those of New Testament times.

When people become alienated from one another, it is important to search for a healing force. A husband and wife may have a child who can hold them together. Members of an athletic team who don't really like one another will cooperate in the heat of a game. Our faith in God should play such a unifying role among believers. This may seem obvious, but all too often we forget or ignore it.

Christians of various denominations and shades of practice should emphasize shared concepts that are so great and so important that, compared with them, other differences fade into relative insignificance. Our faith should transcend all merely human issues, such as whether we are immersed or sprinkled in baptism, have few or many ordinances, have servant pastors or a hierarchical church with bishops and maybe a pope. We can rise above all this when we come together as common believers, but doing so requires both an elevation in spirit and a degree of personal humility.

The closest fellowship Rosalynn and I have with those outside our family is through the Maranatha Baptist Church. But *church* does not mean just "Maranatha" or "Baptist" or "Protestant"; it is the totality of those united in the love of Christ. The ultimate vision of the church should be as a worldwide community in which all believers are joined. As I have come to know, reaching out to others in the name of God can be one of the most deeply rewarding experiences any person can enjoy.

A Rooted Life

For more than fifty years now, the key factor in my good
life has been my relationship with Rosalynn. Even during
our first date, going to a movie, I knew that she was the girl
I wanted to be my wife. Eight months later, she rejected my
marriage proposal, having promised her father that she
would finish her college work first. I persisted, and, after
going with a number of other boys, she acquiesced. In the
years since then, we have had many joys as well as difficult
times, but a foundation of mutual affection and shared religious faith has helped us survive the challenges to our marriage. There is no doubt that we both have grown in the
process.

For our first seven years, we were a navy family, moving

every year or so from one ship or naval base to another. We lived in Virginia, Connecticut, Hawaii, California, back in Connecticut, and then in upstate New York. Our personal life was narrow and focused on each other, since we had little interest in other couples or in life at the officers' clubs during the all-too-rare times when I was at home. Rosalynn was timid around other people then, and eager to accommodate my wishes. Since I was at sea much of the time, she had the household responsibilities—paying the rent, buying groceries, and caring for the children when they came.

For some reason, I was not always able or willing to talk with Rosalynn about problems or worries related to my ship duty, and she was uncomfortable when I was silent or uncommunicative, concerned that I was displeased with her or was falling out of love. Sometimes she cried, and I became angry and even more withdrawn when I could not see any reason for her tears. Despite our love, it was not always easy for us to adjust to each other.

I'm not sure what caused this discomfort in our relationship. Maybe I inherited a male-dominant role from what I thought as a child was the relationship between my parents. (It was only later that I understood my mother's strong will and how she expressed her views to my father in private and often prevailed.) Another factor was that I lived for at least twenty-five days each month in a completely male environment, onboard ship. The relationships were friendly competition with my peers, compliance with orders from my superiors, and expectation that those junior to me would honor my commands. It was incon-

ceivable to exhibit signs of weakness or even emotions that
were not totally under control. Also, it is likely that I considered Rosalynn's household and family responsibilities
relatively insignificant compared with mine.

Our most intense crisis came when my father died. I was
an ambitious young submarine officer, heading the pre-
commissioning crew of the USS *Sea Wolf*, one of the first
two nuclear-powered submarines being designed and built
under the supervision of the legendary Adm. Hyman Rickover. This was the choice assignment in the navy, and I was
clearly destined for a successful career, with promotions
likely to be coming as early as navy regulations would
allow.

I secured a two-week leave from Admiral Rickover to
visit my father and spent this time by Daddy's bedside and
making some calls on old friends around Plains. I was
amazed to discover the extensive nature of my father's contributions to the lives of our neighbors. Dozens of black
and white friends came to our door, greeted me almost as a
prodigal son who had come home, and described what my
father meant to them. These visitors were grieved for him
and our family because he could not live more than another
few weeks, but they were also wondering what they would
do without him.

The extent of my father's charitable giving surprised me
and all of my family. His benevolence had been largely
secret and was only revealed by these people coming to
visit us during the weeks before and after his death. The
principal of the school told us that when any children were
approaching graduation and didn't have proper clothes for

the ceremony, Daddy would always buy them. We discovered that for almost twenty years he had sent a monthly check for twenty-five dollars to a family in town because the husband and father had died. That was a lot of money in those days.

Much of my father's generosity had occurred during the Depression years, when we and our neighbors had little or no money. In 1935, for example, the farmers had to depend on three sources of income: cotton, peanuts, and hogs. Cotton was selling for five cents a pound, and peanuts and hogs for one cent a pound—far below the costs of production. For a farmer to work an acre of peanuts meant buying or saving seed, breaking the land, cultivating it at least seven times, plowing up and shaking dirt from the peanuts, putting them on stacks, letting them dry, threshing them, and hauling them to market. All of this yielded a *gross* income of seven dollars an acre. So throughout our community and much of the rural South, there was virtually no money. In a world like this, my father's charitable acts were all the more remarkable.

He was also deeply involved in every aspect of our town's social and political life. He served on the school and hospital boards, he was a church deacon and taught the junior Sunday school class, and he held a seat in the state legislature. Several times each year, he would haul a truckload of farmers down to the agricultural college at Tifton, about a hundred miles from Plains, so they could learn in one-day training courses how to build better fences or fishponds or how to grow better peanuts or make more cotton.

The diversity of my father's life impressed me deeply—

how he utilized what talent he had in an extraordinarily broad way. I was working hard in the navy, devoting all my talent and ability to learning how to build and operate atomic submarines, and I was proud of what I had accomplished. But I now began to feel that this was a narrowly focused life. The basic question I asked as I reflected on my father's passing was: Whose life is more important in the eyes of God—mine or his?

On the way back to my navy duties in Schenectady, New York, knowing that my father had only a few days to live, I could not erase these memories from my mind, or the question of how the significance of his life compared with my own, even if my highest career ambitions would be realized. I had been committed to the navy since I was a little child, never giving any serious thought to an alternative career. Now I felt I was faced with a completely unexpected question: Should I resign from the U.S. Navy and return to spend the rest of my life in the little town of Plains?

Without telling Rosalynn that I was even considering such a decision, I began to weigh all the major factors. Very important was a feeling of disloyalty to Admiral Rickover and the embryonic nuclear submarine program. The navy had made a tremendous investment in my training and special graduate instruction in nuclear technology. Although I had performed all my assigned duties to the best of my ability, I still felt, at that time, that I was the debtor in the relationship.

Another consideration was that Rosalynn and I had no money, except for some war bonds that we had bought each month out of our relatively small navy salary. I never considered what my father's estate might be or for whom he might have provided in a will. The natural presumption was that everything would go to my mother, and the maximum that any of us children might receive would be a one-fifth interest. Also, after eleven years in the navy, including my time at Annapolis, I knew very little about farming or any other commercial enterprise.

In the navy, we lived our own lives, relatively isolated as a family except for the loose friendships we formed with other navy couples. I think this may have been one of the attractions of the navy life for Rosalynn, who saw her role as the focal point around which our three boys and I revolved. She had not reached her nineteenth birthday when we were married and began our lives as a navy couple. Later, when we spent a few days at home on leave, she claimed that she was still treated as a child by our families. So as a navy wife, she relished her independence, quite different from what she imagined she would have if we moved back into a tiny community where our two mothers were likely to be dominant.

On the other hand, I missed having a religious dimension in my life. Although Rosalynn and I occasionally went to the most convenient Protestant or Catholic church services, usually on naval bases, I didn't feel that I was maintaining any significant commitment to my Christian faith. By contrast, I had been profoundly affected by the sense of a large, close-knit Christian family during my last visit to Plains. There was a genuine outpouring of sympathy, love, and sharing during Daddy's terminal illness that reminded me of my early days in the community. Also, looking at the diversity of my father's activities, I became convinced that my own life would be broadened and not restricted if I went back home.

The overriding issue in this torturous decision was how I wanted to spend the rest of my life. Should I be focused on a promising and honorable career as a professional naval officer, serving my country while working on the cutting edge of science and technology? Or did I want to embark on an almost totally unpredictable future, in a small town among people I had not known for more than twelve years? I continued to face this momentous decision alone. Prayer came naturally to me, and I repeatedly asked God to give me wisdom in assessing all the factors involved.

Over the period of a few days, the balance of advantages became increasingly weighted in my mind in favor of going back home, and by the time I shared the proposal with Rosalynn my decision was made. Rosalynn rebelled in every possible way, but I was adamant. Her resentment was bitter and persistent. However, the intensity and duration of her objections did not deter me from submitting my resignation. A few weeks later, after my father's death and after my resignation from the navy had been accepted, we drove from Schenectady to Plains. Except for our three noisy boys in the backseat, we made the long trip in almost complete silence.

My decision to leave the navy and return home was a crucial event in the life of my family and in my personal and spiritual growth. In time, it led to a deepening of my understanding of and commitment to my religious faith, as well as to the kind of career, both public and private, that I've chosen to follow ever since. But to understand fully this decision and the effects it has had on my life, you need to know something more about the moral framework I originally inherited from my family and my community. This set of principles, rooted in my Christian faith, has both shaped me and been shaped by my personal experiences, and it remains to this day a central element of my identity.

It is difficult for any of us to assess our own habits and actions objectively. Without a set of guidelines, it is not possible to acknowledge and correct the mistaken beliefs and habits that tend to become a way of life.

In my life, there has been a series of codes of conduct by which my activities could be both shaped and judged. They began with my home life and the standards established by my parents, and moved outward in widening circles to encompass my service in the navy, my years as a businessman and citizen in Plains, my political career, and my work after leaving public office. I've found few serious incompatibilities among the ethical codes I encountered along the way; each step tended to expand and strengthen the preceding ones. Some might consider politics an exception, but this is not the case. Contrary to popular opinion, for me and most others in political life, moral principles are actually very high. I'm sure that I did some things that would have displeased my parents or my superior officers if they had been aware of them, but their potential approval or disapproval always provided a framework within which I tried to live.

We all must choose the "guiding lights" that we want to follow. It's easy to set our sights lower. In the navy, I could do my duty and tell the truth but had no real reason or opportunity to be involved in voluntary community activities that would improve the lives of others. If business-people follow just the normally accepted practices of the commercial and professional world, they have little incentive to be concerned about the well-being of those with whom they have no dealings. Truth, justice, and loyalty are virtues common to these spheres and to politics, but rarely are included the additional principles of kindness, humility, compassion, forgiveness, mercy, or sacrificial love.

For all of us, particularly people of faith, there is a higher expectation, as expressed for me by Jesus: "All things whatsoever you would that men should do to you, do you even so to them; for this is the law and the prophets" (Matthew 7:12). A similar standard is set in most religious traditions. As described in the Gospels, Jesus demonstrated in his life how this rule should be put into practice. For Christians, it is not just one of the general rules of our religion but *the* rule concerning our personal behavior.

There are many *unenforceable* standards in our private lives, with only self-imposed incentives to comply with them. If we are interested in lives that excel, we will wish to do more than just obey the law. How do we act when there is no accountability for what we do? What restrains us from being rude to others, ignoring the plight of needy people, giving false information when it's to our advantage, abusing a defenseless person, promulgating damaging gossip, holding a grudge, or failing to be reconciled after an argument? These are things for which we will not be punished, and therefore the fear of retribution is missing as a motivation.

Where can we find an element of transcendence in establishing our own ideals and habits? We are all constrained to balance what we actually are with the image we want to display. We learn to bridge this gap by self-delusion ("I really believe this must be true") or by rationalization ("I didn't mean to say that, and besides, it didn't do any harm"). But if we aspire to grow as human beings, we should struggle to close the gap by making our inner selves truer reflections of our own highest values, which, for me, grow from my Christian faith. In fact, most of the beautiful acts of Jesus as recounted in the Gospels do not relate to compliance with existing laws; they were extraordinary because he reached beyond what was required or expected.

What is the standard by which we make a difficult choice when morality or fairness is concerned? Although Christians consider the Bible the best guide to our life's priorities, it is certainly not easy to apply biblical teachings to every act in our modern lives. So all of us develop other rules through habit and experience. When I was a child, the expectations of my father and mother shaped the framework of my "proper" life, and they were also the judges of my performance.

My father was my idol, and provided the example for me

in work habits, the treatment of others in business dealings, community service, accomplishments in competitive
sports, and the recreational activities of a man. Everyone in
our community respected him in all these facets of life. No
one worked harder or had more innovative ideas.

Although I did well in athletic competition in school, I
never equaled my father—at least until I left home for college and the navy—on the tennis court, off the diving
board, on the pitcher's mound, catching fish, or shooting a
gun. (Today I think I could hold my own with him as
a marksman and could even outdo him with a fly rod.)

Daddy accepted the racial segregation of the South as a
way of life. However, he was known to treat both his
employees and his customers, regardless of race, equally
and with meticulous honesty. If an associate had a bad crop
or family trouble, Daddy was both helpful and extremely
generous. But he had little patience with anyone who fell
short of his own standards, and he was unforgiving when
someone lied to him or tried to cheat on a settlement.

After I returned home from the navy, I tried to assume
most of the voluntary projects that my father had under-
taken, and I soon discovered how burdensome they were.
In addition to the duties I've already mentioned, he had
been active in the Plains Lions Club and was a leader in the
protection and promotion of the rural electrification
system. In effect, many of my goals in civilian life were his
accomplishments, including the beginning of my political
career as a member of the Georgia legislature.

* * *

My father had also taught me what it means to live under strict discipline. Sometimes I was deeply resentful when he punished me, but I knew where I stood, what was expected of me, and the consequences of disobeying the rules.

Once when I was fishing with a friend on the creek nearest our home, we caught the biggest snapping turtle we'd ever seen. We wanted to show it to my parents, so we suspended it from a sapling and started home through the swamp and woods in the middle of the afternoon. We walked through a slow drizzle until after sundown, when we finally saw some tracks, which we were distressed to discover were our own! Realizing that we were lost, we dropped the turtle and concentrated on walking in a straight line. Then the skies cleared and we saw Venus, an evening star at the time, and walked westward by its guidance, in as straight a line as possible through the trees, vines, and swampy ground. I was thankful for my father's training about the more prominent heavenly bodies.

I had mixed emotions. The thing I wanted most was to see my daddy, but that was also what I feared most, realizing that we had violated all the woodsmen's techniques he had taught me. I also knew he would have mounted a search party when we did not return home.

We finally saw lights, which turned out to be in a farmer's cabin about ten miles from our house. Luckily, he had a mule and wagon, and volunteered to carry us home. Too exhausted to walk any farther, we accepted his offer. After traveling for a couple of miles, we met Daddy in his pickup.

We rode six miles over the dirt roads without speaking, my father obviously displeased. He turned to me when we arrived at home and said, "I thought you knew more about the woods than to get lost." Then he reached out to me, and I rushed to embrace him. I knew I deserved to be chastised, but just being in my father's arms was one of my most joyful and memorable experiences. For a few hours, without either of us knowing where the other was, there had been a vacuum in our lives.

My mother set a different kind of standard for me. She served as a registered nurse, and we saw her ministry among the poor families in our community. She worked almost full-time during the Depression years, either twelve-hour days for four dollars or twenty-hour days for six dollars. Between her regular care for private patients, she served as a volunteer medical practitioner—virtually a family doctor—for the extremely poor families who lived in our rural community of Archery. With a group of women helpers, she made additional income each autumn by harvesting pecans from the trees on our farm.

Mama refused to recognize the strict racial segregation of our South Georgia community and throughout her life was considered by some of our neighbors somewhat strange concerning this issue. Even as a child, I could detect a difference between my mother and other people in how she addressed the integration question. In our community this was not a public issue in the 1930s and 1940s, and the unspoken racial customs and subtleties were rigidly observed. But Mama often disobeyed these rules. She would never assume an attitude of superiority toward the black women who worked alongside her in harvesting, shelling, and preparing pecans for market. As a nurse, if anything, she gave our poorest and most needy farm neighbors—usually black—her highest priority.

In those days black people when visiting white people did not go to their front door. The most distinguished resident of Archery was William Johnson, who served five midwestern states as a bishop in the African Methodist Episcopal Church. Such a man was not about to come to a back door. Instead, he would have his driver park his Cadillac or Packard in the front yard and blow the horn. The strange niceties of the day were observed when my father would go out to talk to him.

However, a problem developed after the bishop's son Alvan went to Harvard to study. When he returned home on vacation, he would come to our front door and be received by my mother, who was eager to hear of his experiences in an Ivy League school. If he was home, Daddy would simply leave the front room and ignore the fact that Alvan had made this unprecedented entry. I never knew of any words between my parents on the subject, but they may have discussed it in private—without changing their ways.

My parents and my father's brother and his wife always took their vacations during baseball season, and would travel to a different major league city each year to attend as many ball games as possible. It just happened that they were present in 1947 when Jackie Robinson broke the major league color barrier by playing his first game with the Brooklyn Dodgers. At that moment, Mama became an avowed admirer of Branch Rickey, the general manager who had boldly signed Robinson, and she remained an avid supporter of the Dodgers throughout her life. She stayed up late at night to listen to their West Coast games after they moved to Los Angeles. After Mama's death, we found a gift from the team in her closet, carefully preserved—an entire Dodger uniform, including cleats.

When asked by a news reporter about the origin of her "liberal" attitude on the race issue, Mama explained that it came from her father. When she was a teenager, around 1915, she worked in the Richland post office, where Grandpa was the postmaster. He refused to make any racial distinctions on his job, and, amazingly for those days, he even invited black officials and other visitors to eat lunch with him in one of the rooms of the post office.

My father died in 1953, before the civil rights movement really affected the South, but I have no doubt that Mama's attitude made the acceptance of racial integration much easier for us children, and for others in the community. After her death, some of her friends told me that at their weekly poker games, and at more public social affairs, they were always careful not to tell any jokes or make any remarks that had a racial connotation—out of respect for Mama.

When my parents' influence was divergent or after I was an adult, I absorbed guidance and experience from other sources. Where race was concerned, that source was service in the navy.

It was only after I entered the navy in my late teens that

I came to understand that black and white people should be treated with complete equality. At first, I did not share this new belief with my family. Coming home for brief periods of leave every year or two, I wanted the reunion with my parents to be pleasant and harmonious, and I quickly discovered that the benefits of racial integration on a submarine were not a subject I could discuss freely without a confrontation with my father.

My first personal experience with total racial integration was at the U.S. Naval Academy, when a young student became the first African-American to join the brigade. His name was Wesley Brown, and he was two classes behind me. Although Midshipman Brown was not in my battalion, he and I both ran cross-country. My primary memory of him is that he was always judged by his performance—and he always crossed the finish line ahead of me. A few members of my senior class attempted to find ways to give him demerits so that he would be discharged, but the senior officers at Annapolis investigated every allegation, and Brown's good performance prevailed.

Later, President Harry S Truman ordered an end to racial discrimination in all the armed services, a directive that was honored, so far as I ever knew, without dissension in the navy ranks. On submarines, with the officers and crew required to live much more closely and intimately than on most surface ships, we related easily without any racial incidents.

Once our ship, the USS *K-1*, went into Nassau in the Bahamas for a few days of rest between long periods of undersea training. The governor-general sent a message inviting us to attend a ball the next evening. Our crew members were all excited when his aide reported that a number of young ladies would also be invited. I was on duty the next afternoon, when the aide returned to tell us that, of course, the invitation applied only to the white crewmen. When I delivered this message to the captain, he assembled everyone in the mess hall and informed the crew. We voted unanimously to reject the terms of the invitation and received permission to compose a message in response to the Bahamian officials. After deleting the expletives, the captain had it delivered.

Although the values I absorbed from my father and mother were different, each of my parents shaped me in a way I've never outgrown. I always remember a comment by Judge Elbert Tuttle, one of the great jurists of our country. A Republican appointed by President Dwight Eisenhower, he made some of the most definitive and courageous rulings on civil rights during the troubled segregation days in Georgia. When he retired, he was interviewed by Walter Cronkite, who said, "Judge Tuttle, I understand you've never drunk whiskey." And the judge said, "That's right, I've never in my life tasted an alcoholic drink." Cronkite asked, "Why not?" and the judge gave a simple reply: "Because my mama told me not to."

Similarly, because of my father's strong influence, I have never smoked. Daddy smoked two or more packs of cigarettes a day, beginning as a young army officer during World War I, when Americans first adopted the habit on a large scale. With our government's approval, the tobacco companies had contributed free cigarettes to soldiers. On several occasions he tried, unsuccessfully, to quit. In those days, tobacco advertising was even promoting cigarettes as means to better health, endorsed by doctors, so Daddy had no way of knowing that they would ultimately cause his early death. But he resented the grip of a habit he could not break.

When I was about twelve years old, Daddy called me into the bathroom, closed the door, and said he had a very serious subject to discuss with me. This was an unprecedented and sobering experience, and I was very nervous. Then he said he didn't want me to smoke until I was twenty-one years old, and I agreed, with great relief. I kept my promise until my twenty-first birthday, when I was a midshipman. I bought a pack of cigarettes and took one puff, didn't like it, gave the others away, and never smoked another cigarette. I didn't know until years later what the tobacco companies have always known, that people are not likely to become addicted to tobacco unless they begin smoking at an early age.

This past winter a young friend and I were visiting a tobacco farmer in South Georgia. When the farmer congratulated my friend for ignoring the "propaganda" and lighting up a cigarette, the young man described in an anguished voice his knowledge of the consequences of his smoking, saying, "My wife and I realize that our little child can never be a long-distance runner, and she may have more serious health problems. She's already breathed too much of our smoke."

This has been a tragic element in my life, since both my parents and all my siblings have smoked and died of cancer. One of the great worries that Rosalynn and I share is that some of our children still smoke cigarettes. Despite their best efforts, including scientific and medical counseling, they have not broken free from this affliction.

Although my father was clearly the head of our family, as I noted earlier, I've come to realize how much strength he derived from my mother.

As a young farm boy, I remember my father, though confident in his own ability, being deeply concerned about the future of his crop. He would go out in the yard at night, and we would peek through the front door to see him walking up and down, looking at the sky. Everything he owned, everything he could borrow, was invested in the growing corn, cotton, and peanuts in our fields. If it didn't rain enough, we wouldn't make a very good crop yield, but even worse would be too much rain. Then the Bermuda grass and nut grass couldn't be controlled with hand hoes and mule-drawn plows, and the crop would be totally lost.

Daddy was filled with worry, but as a strong and proud man he didn't share it much with the family. He never said, "I'm really concerned about the rain," but when he came back in the house, my mother would often say, "Earl, everything's going to be all right." Her quiet words meant a lot to him.

My mother's example also showed me that we are never too old to learn. I lecture at a number of colleges and often meet students and others their age who think they know it all and who really have closed their hearts and minds to expansion. But every morning when my eighty-five-year-old mother got out of bed, she was probing for answers, eager to learn more about the people in the Plains community, the Brooklyn Dodgers and baseball strategy, American politics, what was going on in India, or how to make a better pecan crop.

In this constant probing for new information, she differed from my father. When I would come home from life on a navy submarine, my very busy father would ask me just a few questions. He always called me Hot. He'd say, "Hot, are you getting along all right?" I'd say, "Yes, sir." "You need anything?" I'd say, "No, sir." "You like the navy still?" "Yes, sir." And that would be about it.

By contrast, Daddy's brother Alton had my mother's curiosity. I'd go down to Plains Mercantile Co. and talk to my uncle, and he would stand behind his chest-high desk and ask me questions for two hours, perhaps interrupted by a customer or two. By the time we finished talking, he would know all about my submarine, how many people were on it, what kind of food we ate, where we got freshwater at sea, how often I bathed, the money I made every month, the difference between Soviet and American subs—things like that.

Since my father was the dominant force in our family, it was not until several years after his death that Mama began to expand her life beyond our small community. She first joined her older sister and served as housemother for a fraternity at Auburn University. Then she helped organize and operate a nursing home for the elderly in Blakely, Georgia.

One day while at home in Plains, she saw a television advertisement calling for Peace Corps volunteers, stating, "Age is no barrier." She put in an application, requesting only that she be assigned to "a place where people are dark-skinned and desperately in need." As a registered nurse, she was sent to Vikhroli, a small village near Bombay, India, to work in a nationwide program of family planning.

Mama had great difficulty using the Marathi language in her discussions with mostly illiterate people about family planning, including birth control techniques. Finally, she decided to memorize a few words at a time and record each phrase when it was comprehensible. Then she put these together and delivered her recorded message while she hid behind a screen and wiggled some puppets she had made. Although somewhat successful, this was not the best use of her nursing abilities, and the local doctor recruited her to work part-time in his clinic. With permission from the wealthy owners of the village, she was soon working with him full-time.

Mama felt so deeply about these Indian people that she gave them all the food that we would ship to her from home. She was paid a very few dollars each month by the Peace Corps, and she spent all of it on medicine for the clinic.

She lost thirty-five pounds while she was in Vikhroli and returned home in a wheelchair. It would seem that my mother gave up more than she got, that she made a real sacrifice in going to India. But I can tell you that it enriched and transformed her life. After Mama came back at the age of seventy, she made more than 500 speeches. She became famous because of her humor and total frankness, and she always used her own experiences to convince audiences that all of us can have new and greater lives, no matter how old we are, if we're willing to take a chance on something exciting and unpredictable. That, too, is part of the moral framework my parents gave me.

CHAPTER THREE

Finding Peace at Home

As I've said, during the early years of our marriage, I was very reluctant to let Rosalynn know when I had an unresolved problem or was in trouble. I'm not proud to admit that, as far as education and knowledge of public affairs was concerned, I considered myself superior to her, and I supposed she shared this opinion. I didn't want her to know that I was vulnerable to doubt and failure, and both in the navy and when we started our business I did not share everything with her.

Even as late as 1962, when I ran for the Georgia state senate, I agonized over the decision by myself and told Rosalynn I was going to file the qualifying papers only when she asked why I was putting on Sunday pants on a workday. As time went on, however, I came to recognize her wisdom and sound judgment, and what a great relief it was to have both of us seeking answers or solutions. Now it is almost inconceivable to me that she was not intimately involved in every significant decision of my life, as she has been for the past thirty years.

In the fall of 1953, when I left the navy after my father's death, we came home to Plains with three boys, the oldest in the first grade. Rosalynn had her hands full. We lived in a tiny apartment in a public housing project. I struggled alone with our farm supply business, and the first year we had one of the worst droughts in history. None of the farmers could pay their bills. After investing all our savings and what I could borrow in an inventory of seed, fertilizer, and other supplies, we finished 1954 with a total income of less than $300 and a heavy debt. I had to buy more inventory, but my application for a $10,000 loan from the local bank was rejected, unless my mother or uncle would guarantee my note. I refused to ask them, and eventually I secured a small line of credit from the company whose fertilizer I was selling. The next year, 1955, was better, and we had a profit of almost $3,000.

As was the case for most people in Plains, our church became the center of our lives. Almost immediately, Rosalynn and I began teaching Sunday school, the junior girls and boys respectively, between nine and twelve years old. In addition, I was director of the Royal Ambassadors, a Baptist equivalent of the Boy Scouts, and I instructed the boys both in outdoor experiences and about Christian missions. The name of the group came from 2 Corinthians 5:20: "Now then we are ambassadors for Christ, as though God was making his appeal through us." I also formed a Boy Scout troop and was scoutmaster, and Rosalynn was den mother for the Cub Scouts.

The disharmony between me and Rosalynn over our return to Plains and abandonment of navy life slowly dissipated as we became involved in community affairs. But then another problem developed. My farm warehouse customers threatened us with a boycott because we were seen as too liberal on the issue of racial desegregation. Although I didn't know which of my immediate neighbors or farm customers were members of the Ku Klux Klan, almost all the white men in Plains belonged to the White Citizens' Council. This was a loose organization publicly sponsored by most of Georgia's political leaders, including the incumbent U.S. senators, the governor, and other officials of the state and local governments. They collected annual dues of five dollars, issued membership cards, and had one or two public meetings each year. No one except the top leaders ever knew what happened to the dues money.

The Council members always professed to be nonracist and peaceful in their purposes, but they were strongly against racial integration. It was understood that a line was being drawn among white citizens concerning the civil rights movement. The two Council leaders in Plains were the railroad depot agent and the town marshal, both of whom knew everyone and had time to sign up members, keep records of local dues collected, and deliver pamphlets and notices. When they first called on me in my warehouse office, I told them I was not inclined to join the Council. That night I discussed the issue with Rosalynn, and we agreed that we could not yield to the community pressure, even if the decision might severely reduce our already marginal income from the warehouse. When the marshal came back to see me, I informed him that I did not intend to be a member. He told me I was making a serious mistake and claimed that every other white man in town had signed up.

I did not hear anything more until, one day in the early summer of 1955, about twenty of my best customers came to see me. They were respected men whom I knew well, longtime friends of my father. The spokesman for the group, whose name was Paul, said they realized that I had been in the navy for a long time, away from the South, and had worked on ships where the crews were integrated. They were sure I was not completely familiar with some of the changes that had taken place in my absence.

He then quietly outlined the segregationist principles with which I was, of course, thoroughly familiar, including the supposed biblical foundation for the separation of races, potential damage to the quality of our schools if black and white students were together, and eventual destruction of the white race through the intermarriages that would inevitably occur. He reminded me about the prominent politicians who were leaders of the group and added that the Council members were equally concerned about the welfare of our black neighbors, among whom, he claimed, only a few radicals, mostly outsiders, wanted to make any change. He said that the Council was against any form of violence and that they were in no way connected with the Klan or other militant organizations.

He pointedly reminded me that all of them had traded with my father, had fond affection for our family, and knew that I was struggling with my new business after the previous disastrous year. They had decided among them to pay the annual dues for me, but they needed my signature on the membership form. There was no need for me to play an active role in the organization.

I believed then and believe now that most of the men had what they thought were my best interests at heart and were trying to protect me from criticism. It was a very difficult moment, and I knew that I was facing the prospect of losing a substantial portion of my trade in the surrounding community, but I decided to resolve the issue once and for all.

In a somewhat shaky voice, I told the group how much I appreciated their trying to be helpful and their loyalty in continuing to be my customers. I understood their arguments and concerns, some of which also troubled me. However, I had decided not to join the White Citizens' Council and could not change my mind. It was not the payment of dues that was a problem; even with their money I could not contribute to an organization in which I did not believe.

Paul voiced his regret at my response, and the group left without any expressions of anger. For several weeks, very few customers came to trade with me. Fortunately, this was at the beginning of a dormant period in our annual business cycle, shortly after the crops were "laid by" and about

two months before harvesttime. During this time, I
thought a lot about leaving Plains and getting a job with
some large company involved in the young but expanding
nuclear power industry. In fact, I had standing offers from
General Dynamics and General Electric, the two companies with which I had been working on the building of the
nuclear submarine *Sea Wolf.* I did not discuss this question
again with Rosalynn, though, because I really did not
intend to leave home.

One by one, I visited the men who had come to see me
and found them to be much less concerned individually
than they had seemed in the group that day. In fact, some
of them resented the pressure that had been put on them to
join the Council.

This was a serious crisis, but it brought Rosalynn and
me even closer together. She began to help me at the warehouse, keeping the books, sending out monthly bills, and,
after a year or two, settling up with a few of our customers for their entire year's trade. Our hard work and the
slowly improving racial attitudes in Georgia let us survive
financially.

The following year, I was chosen by the grand jury to
serve on the Sumter County School Board, in the position
formerly held by my father. This was a prestigious appointment, since the state constitution gives school boards
almost complete authority over the education system,
including all personnel decisions, the assignment of students, purchase of school buses and other equipment and
supplies, construction and maintenance of buildings, and

the right to levy adequate property taxes to finance the operation. In Georgia, little official interference was permitted in these decisions, even from the governor's office. Following the Supreme Court's 1954 decision in *Brown v. Board of Education*, which struck down school segregation laws in all states, these local school boards were the focal points for decisions about racial integration. We five (white) men and our counterparts throughout the state had to face this issue, and, although it took more than a decade, each of the 200 local boards of education in Georgia eventually authorized school integration without violence. We avoided the public confrontations between governors and U.S. officials that occurred in Mississippi, Arkansas, and Alabama.

Unfortunately, the overall issue was not resolved easily. For the following fifteen years (and even until today), strong segregation sentiments remained. The influence of the White Citizens' Councils slowly faded in all the Southern states except Mississippi, but in our county the John Birch Society gained a stronghold. In our county seat, Americus, a majority of bankers, doctors, and lawyers were active members. The daily *Times-Recorder* always ran the John Birch column prominently on its editorial page. A number of private schools were organized by white parents who refused to permit their children to be educated with black students.

Strong social and economic pressures were exerted to prevent further integration. The churches, free from government authority, were most immune to change.

There was a widely published photograph of black people kneeling in prayer in front of an Americus church, confronted by a stern line of Methodist stewards with arms crossed, guarding the front door of God's house of worship. As late as 1965, after I had been a Georgia state senator for three years, another boycott was organized against our family business. After our eldest son graduated from high school, the entire family took a three-week summer vacation to Mexico. We traveled without a specific itinerary, often staying in smaller cities, practicing our Spanish, and seeing the sights. When we returned home, I noticed that very few people came to my office as they usually did to buy feed, settle small accounts, or just visit for a while.

After a few days, one of our relatives told me that he had been visited by some prominent John Birchers who informed him where we had supposedly spent the last several weeks. I soon discovered that they had gone to the county courthouse, examined the public agricultural records, obtained a list of everyone who had ever sold peanuts to us, and then visited them all to urge that they no longer deal with our warehouse. Their story was that we had visited a communist training camp in northern Alabama for a month, learning how to expedite racial integration in the South. These were some of the most successful leaders in our county, including the president of a large insurance agency and the man who had served in the state legislature for eight years, filling the seat my father had held.

I immediately confronted these two men, who had concocted the story. Both of them claimed they had irrefutable evidence that their information was correct. It was only after I returned with hotel receipts and other records from places in Mexico that they grudgingly admitted I had not been trained by communists. Then, as had been the case ten years earlier, I had to visit my customers one at a time in order to defuse the crisis.

Most of our friends who were racial moderates, including the president of our college, the owner of the only local radio station, and the county attorney, were forced to leave the community. We survived the boycott and other pressures because of several advantages. Although it was not often mentioned, there was a clear social advantage in belonging to one of the old, pioneer families. Buried in family cemeteries near Plains are Rosalynn's and my ancestors who were born in the eighteenth century. Their many descendants were devoted members of the Baptist, Methodist, and Lutheran churches, and my father and his brother had been quite active in community affairs. My uncle was mayor of Plains for twenty-eight years. Perhaps equally important in our determination to stay was that our family ties were too strong to break. Ancestral lands and five generations of neighboring kinfolks were much more difficult to relinquish than a law practice, a radio station, or even the top position at the local college.

In a way, our approach to the race issue was also excused because of my mother's acknowledged "eccentricity" and because we were known to have spent a number of years in the navy. Furthermore, by the time of the boycott, Rosalynn and I were personally rooted in Plains. I was deeply immersed in our new career, and I had no doubt that I had made the right decision on leaving the U.S. Navy. Our church life provided a foundation for almost everything we did. I had been elected a deacon and was teaching the Sunday school class that my father had taught. Increasingly, our leaving home was inconceivable.

I was really enjoying the opportunities for me to use all of my abilities in our growing warehouse business, in producing on our farm some of the finest seed peanuts in Georgia, in helping to preserve the public school system in the early throes of racial integration, and in serving as Boy Scout master, on the local library board, and on the hospital authority. I was making a rapid climb up the hierarchy of Lions International to district governor, responsible for fifty-four Southwest Georgia clubs. I helped to pull seven counties into a regional group to share our opportunities for development, and I was one of the organizers and the first president of the Georgia Planning Commission. It makes me tired now to look back on it all, but then it was giving me a full and gratifying life.

Plains was and is a wonderful place to live. As in all Southern communities, its white people were faced with a quandary during the civil rights days, but they struggled through the ordeal and ultimately made the right decision. The "professional" segregationist leaders who influenced both the legal system and most of the religious congregations eventually faded into the background. With each passing year during the 1950s and 1960s, more and more citizens in our town came to understand that "separate but equal" was compatible with neither the U.S. Constitution nor the teachings of Jesus Christ.

However, divisions on the race issue remained throughout this time, and it was natural for Rosalynn and me to seek companions who shared our basic views. Through silent agreement, we broke off relations with a few farm couples with whom we had earlier spent a lot of time. Two of them were relatives of ours, and there was an obvious coolness when we attended the same family reunions. As late as 1977, while I was living in Washington, our congregation split, roughly along Baptist political lines, with about twenty-five of the more "moderate" members leaving to form a new church. It has now grown to about fifty families, and our more conservative "mother" church is also thriving.

In some things, we just have to be patient. The Bible says, "For you have need of patience, that, after you have done the will of God, you might receive the promise" (Hebrews 10:36). As Paul told the Romans, "Be devoted to one another in brotherly love. Honor one another above yourselves. Be joyful in hope, patient in affliction, faithful in prayer" (Romans 12:10, 12). Now, after two more decades, most of the divisions have healed. We shake hands and talk to everyone at the reunions, and the Plains churches share fifth Sunday night services and visit each other during our respective revival weeks and on other special occasions.

*   *   *

During these years, Rosalynn and I formed close friendships with a few other couples, mostly farmers, and began a fairly intense social life, almost exclusively on Saturday nights. For most of the year, all of us worked from dawn to dusk, six days a week, and we enjoyed the small private parties that became an integral part of our lives. Sometimes we would come home long after midnight, take a short nap, study and teach our Sunday school lessons, and then sleep during the afternoon, getting ready for another week of work. On occasion, we had bitter arguments, based on jealousy or mutual criticism of behavior at parties. By this time, we had been married for ten years.

Throughout our marriage, despite different interests, the imperfection of both partners, mistakes made, even irresolvable differences of opinion, love has prevailed. There have been a number of times when we were angry at each other and I had to teach a Bible lesson with Rosalynn in the class. It is hardly possible for a quarrel to survive when I am teaching a Scripture such as "Love suffers long, and is kind; love envies not; love vaunts not itself, is not puffed up, does not behave itself unseemly, seeks not her own, is not easily provoked, thinks no evil; rejoices not in iniquity, but rejoices in the truth; bears all things, believes all things, hopes all things, endures all things" (1 Corinthians 13:4–7).

We have not been immune from the problems that threaten most couples. There is no doubt that some of these family conflicts would have been serious enough to threaten our marriage were it not for the sustaining religious faith that we have shared. We have never been to counselors or psychiatrists, or even discussed our differences with a close friend or our pastor. But for both me and Rosalynn there have been religious and spiritual criteria by which we could assess our own actions and honor our marriage vows. Also, there has always been a third party, Jesus Christ, with whom we could share our most troubling crises through prayer—often individually, sometimes together.

In 1987, Rosalynn and I wrote a book as coauthors called *Everything to Gain*. It dealt with the traumatic events of my presidential reelection loss in 1980, finding ourselves in debt, and returning after ten years to an empty house with our last child, Amy, soon to leave home. We attempted to describe our experiences and offer advice to others who face similar difficult passages in their lives.

Writing this book was one of the most severe threats to the harmony of our forty-one-year marriage. It was fairly easy for Rosalynn and me to agree on 97 percent of the text, but we found the other 3 percent impossible. In our struggles to describe precisely what had happened and how we had reacted to each event, we simply could not concur on language. The adjectives and adverbs were particularly difficult. It soon became impossible for us to communicate directly, so we exchanged increasingly unpleasant comments through our word processors.

In addition, we had different writing methods. I write quite rapidly, while Rosalynn labors over each paragraph. She always considered my writing as a rough draft, while I accused her of acting as though every portion of her text had been delivered on stone tablets from Mount Sinai.

It was only the last-minute refereeing of our editor that saved the book, and, as we said only somewhat jokingly, perhaps our marriage. We finally accepted his suggestion that we divide up the paragraphs on which we could not agree, with mine marked with a "J" and hers with an "R."

We breathed a sigh of relief when our book was published shortly before Christmas, and we began to pull our lives back together. However, we soon found other sources of irritation. One that was particularly troubling was that during each of the increasingly cold winter nights we argued about the temperature of our electric blanket. Whenever I said it was too warm, Rosalynn said it was too cold, and vice versa.

One morning I returned from an overnight trip to New York, and she met me at the front door with a warm hug and a smile. "I think our marriage is saved," she said. "I just discovered that our dual blanket controls have been on the wrong sides of the bed, and each of us was changing the temperature on the other's side."

Over the years, Rosalynn and I have tried a lot of new things together, each of us expanding our interests to include those of the other. We have taken up downhill skiing (when I was sixty-two years old), tennis, mountain climbing, fly-fishing, biking, and Spanish as a second language. We have now had a lot of experience in resolving family disputes, and the proven lack of fragility in our long-term relationship helps us to address even the most unpleasant and difficult subjects with frankness (although sometimes with a high degree of anger). We've certainly never been bored, and on occasion we have found innovative ways to resolve problems.

One of my best gifts to Rosalynn was to resolve a recurring argument. I was very busy at the time, putting the final touches on a book. I went into my study early one morning, turned on my computer, and hit a button that automatically put the date on the screen. There it was: August 18, her birthday, and I hadn't gotten her a present! Rosalynn was still in bed. So I started wondering what I could give her that I didn't have to go down to my cousin Hugh's antiques store to buy. In desperation, I tried to analyze the things that caused trouble in our marriage—in addition to my forgetting anniversaries and birthdays.

One of the things that had created a problem for us for thirty-five years or more was punctuality. I was affected by my training in the navy and, I think, inherited the trait from my father. Whether to meet a train, to attend a baseball game, or to keep an appointment, he was always there long ahead of time. If someone kept him waiting, he had no patience. He would stalk out of a doctor's office if his appointment was delayed for more than ten minutes. Unfortunately, I, too, am uncomfortable if someone keeps me waiting, and if I'm late and inconvenience someone else, I get even more uptight. To the surprise of my campaign workers and some audiences, I even kept to a strict schedule during my political campaigns, in the governor's office, and in the White House.

And so Rosalynn and I had a lot of arguments about being on time. She always claimed that she was never late, and this would be true if judged by the standards of a reasonable person. What should two or three minutes matter between a husband and wife preparing to go to a movie or a party? But I was not reasonable, holding Rosalynn to a standard of absolute precision. Even before our appointed time for departure, I would remind her of the need to leave and would often produce at least a dirty look if I had to wait at the door.

So, reflecting on all this on that morning of her birthday, I wrote a note to her: "Rosalynn, I promise you that for the rest of our marriage, I will never make an unfavorable remark about tardiness." I signed it and gave it to her for a present. So far I've pretty well kept my promise, and she still agrees that it was the best birthday present I ever gave her.

When a man and woman first meet and there seems to be the potential for a bond between them, they explore each other in a cautious, perhaps uncertain way. Maybe the relationship develops into intimacy, families become involved, and a marriage proposal is accepted and consummated. This sounds like a happy ending to a delightful story, but it's just the introduction to a marriage.

What makes a marriage? Is a personal union built or strengthened mainly by dramatic events? I would say no. It's the year-by-year, dozen-times-a-day demonstration of the little things that can destroy a marriage or make it successful. The ability to communicate is most important. In almost every marriage, times arise when the husband and wife look on the same event with different perspectives. If they can talk about their views with honesty and mutual respect—a big if—many problems can be avoided. We have to be willing to forgive, because mistakes are going to be made. There is going to be anger and even, at times, deliberately hurtful words, so understanding and flexibility are required. And it is crucial during times of crisis to maintain an overriding sense of permanence. For Rosalynn and me, the marriage vows have been a powerful stabilizing force. Largely because we consider these pledges inviolable, we have survived our differences now for fifty years.

Rosalynn and I share a page or a chapter in the Bible each night. In addition to what we learn about religion and life, there is an element of self-discipline about this ritual that is beneficial. It also brings us closer together, helping to reconcile a lot of small arguments that would otherwise have carried over until the next day. We alternate reading aloud, most often from a modern Spanish version, with the English text alongside. This gives us the additional benefit of practicing our second language; on occasion I have been able to deliver a fairly comprehensible Sunday morning message from the pulpit in a Latin American country. Even when we are not together, we continue our reading, and we enjoy knowing that we are reading the same Scripture passage.

If we outline the basic elements of a marriage, we see that the same things apply in our relationship with Christ: love, forgiveness, loyalty, flexibility, the admission of mistakes; looking inward; the ability to ask, What is there about my own life that is not acceptable to Christ, and am I willing to change, to repent?

Christians have, in effect, gone through a marriage pledge with Jesus, and it is a form of adultery to violate this pledge by putting anything above the relationship with him. I was reminded of my military and political oaths when I put on my navy uniform or walked by the Rose Garden to the Oval Office each morning. And of course being with Rosalynn is a constant reminder of my pledge and obligations to her. I want to continue developing the same awareness of my commitment to Christ.

Of course, being faithful to God is a way to strengthen ties within my family, in military service, and in political office. It is good for me to remember that I took my oaths "before God" to fulfill all those obligations to the best of my ability.

The way Rosalynn and I have dealt with our children has not been so naturally self-corrective. One of the most difficult challenges for me has been the questioning of my dominant role and the realization of as much equality as possible among all members of the family. My father instilled in me a respect for strict discipline, and, either genetically or through my home environment, I inherited his approach to the raising of children.

I never really questioned this approach to parenthood until our oldest son, Jack, became an adult. One day, while he and I walked through our fields hunting quail, he began to describe to me his deep resentment of the way I had treated him as a growing boy. I was shocked and immediately became defensive. We stopped walking and exchanged heated words about some specific events that he recalled tearfully but that I hardly remembered. I could tell that this was a subject he had discussed with his wife and that his decision to confront me had been very difficult. But I couldn't acknowledge that I had been mistaken in my basic approach all those years—or that my own father had also been overly domineering.

We returned home, unreconciled and extremely uncomfortable. I immediately told Rosalynn what had happened, emphasizing Jack's lack of appreciation for all we had done for him. But together we soon came to realize the legitimacy of much of what Jack had said. When I brought myself to analyze the bonds that existed between my father, me, and my three sons more honestly, I still found it impossible to express them except through a poem.

I Wanted to Share My Father's World

This is a pain I mostly hide,
but ties of blood, or seed, endure,
and even now I feel inside
the hunger for his outstretched hand,
a man's embrace to take me in,
the need for just a word of praise.

I despised the discipline
he used to shape what I should be,
not owning up that he might feel

his own pain when he punished me.
I didn't show my need to him,
since his response to an appeal
would not have meant as much to me,
or been as real.

From those rare times when we did cross
the bridge between us, the pure joy
survives.

> *I never put aside*
the past resentments of the boy
until, with my own sons, I shared
his final hours, and came to see
what he'd become, or always was—
the father who will never cease to be
alive in me.

I was a lot like my father, probably even as a child, and did not find it easy to demonstrate my feelings toward him. As an adult and a father myself, I finally realized that I had a similar relationship with my own sons. Since Jack and his family lived near Chicago, we didn't see them very often after our confrontation in the field, and it was only over a period of several months that we exchanged some brutally frank letters, made some visits, and took a few initiatives toward reconciliation, including my acknowledgment that my level of discipline in raising our boys may have been too high.

In retrospect, I can see that instinctively emulating this autocratic father-son relationship a generation later was a mistake. Times had changed, and growing boys expected and needed more freedom in an age of television and automobiles of their own.

It is not easy for us to give freedom to those we love. Most of us want to be able to rely on an intimate relationship, and we fear that liberation of a spouse or child will destroy our closeness and interdependence. This may mean that ours is a self-centered love, perhaps even relying on psychological domination to hold others close.

As my father dominated my mother, I had the same relationship with Rosalynn in our early years, but during the last forty or more years, we have evolved what is an almost purely equal partnership. This change has come about not from any decision of mine but as a result of Rosalynn's natural strength and ability. In my marriage and in that of my parents, I can see quite clearly the advantages of personal freedom and an absence of subordination of one person by another.

Sometimes the guidance of religious principles is even more valuable within the intimacy of a family than outside. With a spouse, especially one with a strong will, there is a mandatory give-and-take that tends to force frank assessments—and adjustments. Particularly since leaving the political world, where we all faced common challenges together, our family has learned to resolve difficult interpersonal issues by communicating. We have sometimes resorted to frank and disturbing letters, but on most occasions we find some way to approach difficult issues face to face. On a few occasions when it was not possible for me to relate directly to our sons, our daughters-in-law and Rosalynn have been able to resolve potential problems.

When possible during the year, Rosalynn and I try to take a few of our family members with us on interesting trips involving our work, and during each Christmas–New Year's season, we have a family vacation together—all eighteen of us! One or two telephone calls a week also help. Our sons have good and solid families, we have mutual trust and love among us, and so far this has worked.

However, everything is not perfect. Even though we always have a blessing together at mealtimes and take our grandchildren to church when they are visiting us, I can't say that we have been an effective influence on our children with respect to their religious lives. They acknowledge their Christian faith but are not regular members of a church.

Although we feel responsible, we realize that our children must have freedom to run their own lives. Since college, they haven't lived near us or in a close-knit community like ours, where everyone is expected to be active in a church. Also, they dislike the constant squabbling about doctrine and church politics among many Baptists and disagree strongly with some of the more fundamentalist positions of famous preachers. It may be that we were too demanding concerning church attendance when they were children, their suburban lives may have too many other enticements on Sundays, or our personal examples may not have been attractive. We realize that Rosalynn and I had the same slack habits about worship while I was in the navy, and it was only when we came back to Plains that we found church life attractive and gratifying.

All of us feel alone when we disagree with others or face the death of someone we love. I have felt the distress of losing all the members of my childhood family, and have seen two of my sons suffer through the emotional torment of divorce. In such times, the thing that has never changed as a sustaining force has been our religious faith, within which we have been able to find guidance on how best to face a crisis.

With increasing maturity, I have seen more clearly that I must adapt to differences among people, learn to accept the imperfect, understand the fallibilities of ourselves and others, and have mercy—in other words, forgive. Forgiveness is not easy, but it is a goal to be sought, a process that should continue throughout our lives.

More and more, I've come to realize that forgiveness is a basic foundation of my faith. Without the knowledge that I can be forgiven, it would not be possible to face my own shortcomings frankly. Without forgiveness, I could not confess to a God whose standards embody perfection, or learn how to forgive others or myself.

How can I believe God's promises of complete forgiveness? By remembering the teachings of Jesus, and by looking at the lives of biblical characters whose transgressions involved the most terrible of crimes, both against God and against human law.

King David was a poet, a musician, a courageous warrior, and a fine political leader, greatly blessed. But he was also a terrible sinner who did almost everything we can think of to violate the Ten Commandments. Yet he was completely reconciled with God. How was that possible? Through his confession and his turning to God for understanding and repentance: "And David said to the prophet Nathan, 'I have sinned against the Lord.' And Nathan said to David, 'The Lord has put away your sin; you shall not die' " (2 Samuel 12:13).

In the Thirty-second Psalm, David writes, "Happy are those to whom the Lord imputes no iniquity and in whose spirit there is no deceit." David is giving us the lesson he learned in going through the extremes of life, from doubt to faith, from sin to forgiveness, and from guilt to joy.

The most convincing proof of Jesus' forgiveness involved Peter, perhaps the most intriguing disciple, whose life with Christ went through wild swings from approbation to condemnation.

When Jesus asked his disciples who they thought he was, "Simon Peter said, 'You are the Christ, the Son of the living God' " (Matthew 16:16). Just a few minutes later, Peter rejected the idea that his master would have to suffer death on the cross. Jesus turned to him and said, "Get behind me, Satan! You are a stumbling block to me " (Matt. 16:23).

Despite his weakness, his equivocation, and, later, his cowardly betrayal of Christ, Peter was never finally rejected but repeatedly forgiven and reconciled with Jesus. As Jesus prophesied, "You are Peter, the rock on which I will build my church" (Matthew 16:18).

God offers us a mixture of gentleness and discipline, not unlike that of a caring parent. Jesus said, "I did not come to judge the world, but to save the world" (John 12:47).

If we commit a crime or make a serious mistake, we are naturally reluctant to confess, fearing punishment or the condemnation of others. For a Christian, assured of God's mercy, this reluctance need not exist. However, the Bible says that confession and repentance are necessary before we can receive this total forgiveness.

Every now and then, one of my Sunday school lessons is about forgiveness, and it is a difficult subject for me to teach. Almost invariably, a feeling of hypocrisy gnaws at me as I remember people against whom I still hold a grudge. Most of my lingering resentments relate to our time in Washington. In some cases, I have said, "I can't forgive that jerk!" But when I forced myself to consider the original altercations more thoroughly, they usually came to seem somewhat silly—some I couldn't even remember.

Is lasting resentment *ever* justified? Not according to the standards set for us by Christ, who said, "Judge not, that you be not judged" (Matthew 7:1) and "But if you do not forgive others, then your Father will not forgive your transgressions" (Matt. 6:15). In the Lord's Prayer, God's forgiveness of us is conditional: "And forgive us our trespasses, as [or provided] we forgive those who trespass against us" (Matt. 6:12). Peter once asked Jesus, "Lord,

how often shall my brother sin against me and I forgive
him? Up to seven times?" Jesus responded, "No, seventy
times seven" (Matt. 18:21–22).

Teaching these lessons has induced me to correct some
of my mistakes. On a few occasions, I have written letters
to the people involved, saying that I hoped we could be reconciled. Most of the time this has worked, and I've shared
some of the responses with my classes.

There's another step, though, beyond my forgiving
another person and being forgiven by God, and that is forgiveness of myself. If God can forgive us, why can't we
forgive ourselves? A lot of us feel that this promise of total
reconciliation is too good to be true.

Even aside from religion, to be forgiven is extremely
important. Nowadays, many people are, in effect, willing
to pay to have their feelings of guilt explained or forgiven.
A psychiatrist will try to help us comprehend the reasons
for even our grossest behavior, often because of something
our parents did or failed to do when we were little children.
Early mistreatment is sometimes even considered in our
legal system to be an excuse for crimes, including murder.
We may or may not be able to shift blame to our parents,
but at least we can ease our pain or suffering by forgiving
ourselves.

If we live with a permanent feeling of guilt, we are spir-
itually and emotionally crippled. The extreme case is
someone who becomes depressed and commits suicide—
an almost incomprehensible tragedy. A few years ago, my
best friend in Atlanta took his own life, and just as I have

been writing this, a distinguished navy leader took the same action, apparently because he wore on his chest some small symbols of personal valor in combat that he did not deserve. We really need someone who can be judgmental but forgiving, able to accept our warts, our defects. Rosalynn, for instance, doesn't hesitate to provide me with suggestions to do better: "You didn't take enough questions in Sunday school" or "I believe you were too harsh with our son" or "You forgot to thank so-and-so for what she did for us." I cherish having a relationship with Rosalynn that is based on faith and mutual trust and is so intimate that I can reveal myself to her.

I would go a step further and say that if we are not willing to share ourselves with others enough to get beneficial suggestions from them, then we have lost a wonderful way to have better, more exciting, and more fruitful lives. It's through this exchange of criticism, based on mutual understanding and forgiveness, that we are able to grow.

Even among people who are closest, there is a need for repetitive forgiveness. Rosalynn and I are both strong willed and frequently have disagreements, some of them lasting for several days. It is difficult for either of us to admit being at fault. Recently, after a particularly disturbing argument, I decided that we should never let another day end with us angry with each other. I went to my wood shop and cut out a thin sheet of walnut, a little smaller than a bank check. I then carved on it:

Each evening, forever, this is good for an apology—or forgiveness—
as you desire. Jimmy.

So far, I have been able to honor it each time Rosalynn
has presented it to me. And she has!

Leadership and Faith

I served in the U.S. Navy for eleven years, between the ages of eighteen and twenty-nine. These years had a profound influence on me and on the course of my life. In particular, during this time I thought frequently and learned much about the art and discipline of leadership as I rose through the ranks from a sailor obeying the commands of others to a position of authority, responsible for the safety and military effectiveness of many other men.

In the years since then, I have often compared my life as a Christian, as a naval officer, and as a political leader. I find my navy duty and my religious faith to be most closely related. Although I may be idealizing the navy example, I can see a relationship between my service on my first submarine, the USS *Pomfret,* for instance, and my idea of proper service as a Christian. Among the crew of this ship, because of the leadership of the captain, there was eagerness to measure up to strong and firm standards, repentance for mistakes, but confidence in forgiveness— qualities for which people of faith should also strive.

Later, of course, as president and commander in chief, I bore the ultimate military authority in our nation. (Although, as President Harry Truman said, one of the biggest surprises to him was that often when he gave an order from the Oval Office to the government bureaucracy, nothing happened. This is a significant difference between military and civilian authority!) In the White House, I tried to apply the lessons I'd learned about leadership from my varied experiences during the navy years.

As a young midshipman, I was instructed meticulously in a demanding code of conduct. According to my aging copy of *The Bluejackets' Manual,* in the performance of our duties we were "expected to exhibit obedience, knowledge, fighting spirit, reliability, loyalty, initiative, self-control, energy, courage, justice, faith in ourselves, honor, and cheerfulness." But the overarching criterion was truth— absolute truth, which was described as "the *final* test of a man." Any form of lying or dishonesty was justification for immediate dismissal from the Naval Academy. During every one of my eleven years in the U.S. Navy, I knew that my superior officers were judging my compliance with these standards.

Although the navy's image has been tarnished by recent

scandals, such as the Tailhook incident, basic military standards have not changed. One of the advantages of living in our democratic society is that such problems are most often revealed and then corrected. As a young officer, I saw the first break in widespread racial segregation occur at the Naval Academy and on ships; now, perhaps, reports of sexual abuse among naval aviators will help to expose and correct another problem that is much more pervasive in America than was previously acknowledged.

I looked upon the navy rules and regulations as a framework for my performance as an officer, one tried and tested for hundreds of years as the best means to ensure effective roles for my ship and crew. However, there were two limitations on the application of these regulations in my life. One was that they did not extend to my role as a Christian husband and father. The second was that the navy code was sometimes misinterpreted or distorted by the administration and enforcement of my commanding officers.

I had many opportunities to take on additional responsibilities that would contribute to the overall quality of my service. At first, I was an extremely eager officer, taking on as many volunteer duties as I could, including extra study about naval strategy, navigation, astronomy, seamanship, and the more intricate details of the ship's electronic system.

However, my continued zeal in performing these voluntary chores was determined by the satisfaction I derived from them and my respect for those who observed my performance. As we strive to go beyond the "letter of the law" and live up to higher standards of conduct and behavior, the quality of the leadership, guidance, and inspiration we receive becomes especially important.

As a naval officer, I served on four ships and under six captains. The good ships were governed with strict but fair discipline. However, my second captain was a martinet, who exercised his authority in an arbitrary and vindictive way. When the ship approached a port, we never knew whether or when we would be permitted to go ashore to see our families. If some member of the large crew had displeased the captain, there might be several hours of unexplained delay before anyone except the top officers could leave the ship. Morale was extremely low, and there was a smoldering resentment against the captain.

I was on this ship when the 1948 presidential primary election was approaching, and I was interested in politics, studying the news about the Democratic candidates who were challenging the incumbent, Harry Truman, whom I admired. We junior officers had some friendly but heated discussions about the campaign in the wardroom. One day, I was told to report to the captain immediately. When I found him, he was making an inspection of the ship. He didn't speak to me but motioned for me to follow his entourage. I did so for more than an hour, and finally we approached his living quarters. He paused outside his door, called me forward, thrust his flashlight forcefully into my chest, and said, "Either choose the navy or politics." Then he turned and left me standing there.

So far as I remember, these were the only words this

commanding officer ever spoke to me, and this insulting treatment—failing to explain the problem and prodding me physically and with obvious displeasure in front of several other people—I considered to be inexcusable. Less embarrassing but equally important was his condemnation and apparent prohibition of discussing the presidential election.

Life under this commander quickly eroded my sense of commitment to naval service. I soon came to believe that I had made a dreadful mistake in choosing a military career and resolved to resign as soon as my legal obligations were fulfilled. I hung a sign on the bulkhead of my tiny cabin that said, SO WHAT? For me, there were no remaining incentives—not the hope for future rewards, the threat of a negative fitness report, or the approval of the captain—for performance beyond my required duties.

However, before the end of the year, my application for service in submarines was accepted. This was elite duty. Standards of performance were high, and there was a degree of intimacy among the officers and crew members that I had not known before.

On one submarine, I had a captain who created a problem of a different kind. He was always friendly and forgiving, but he seemed more at ease dealing with all his subordinates as equals than with exercising real authority as our commander. This was nice at first, but we soon realized that his apparent benevolence came from a lack of interest in or knowledge about details. He treated all of us as he would wish to be treated by a forgiving superior who knew he didn't perform his duties well. As a result, a general lackadaisical attitude evolved, to the extent that we were not confident of the safety of the submarine, where our lives depended on the proper performance of all members of the crew. Eventually, some of us junior officers discussed the problem with the executive officer, who was second in command. In effect, for the remainder of this captain's tour onboard, he was quietly bypassed in the exercise of discipline.

I had two other fine officers as submarine commanders, but the best captain under whom I ever served was J. B. Williams, Jr., a natural leader. It was he who inspired me as an officer. He was bold and aggressive, pushing our relatively old submarine, the USS *Pomfret*, to its limit with quick dives, fast and deep runs, and steep eruptions to the surface. During war games with Canadian and British destroyers off the shore of China, he would have us emerge from the depths in the midst of their ship formations, taunting them with the realization that we had approached without being detected. He was also a kind and gentle man, and the junior officers and lowliest enlisted men felt a sense of his friendship and knew the captain was protective of their interests. He was strict and clear in his demands on the crew but always ready to forgive mistakes when we made them. Our punishment for errors lay in our remorse for having let him down.

As I've mentioned before, my final commanding officer in the navy was Adm. Hyman Rickover, the father of nuclear power. Rickover was intensely demanding of everyone who worked for him. Anything short of perfection brought severe castigation, but there was never any comment when he could find no fault with our work. No matter how he drove us, though, we all realized that he demanded even more of himself. During the early 1950s, I would sometimes fly with him from the East Coast to visit nuclear reactors in Arco, Idaho, or the Hanford plant near Richland, Washington, where nuclear fuel was refined. Determined to make a good impression, I would resolve to work all the way, a trip that in prejet days required about ten hours. But despite my best efforts, I would have to take a nap or at least rest my eyes, something that Rickover never did.

I admired and respected him without reservation, and believe him to have been the finest engineer who has ever lived. If moored end to end, the nuclear-powered ships built under his close supervision would have stretched for ten miles. Despite being highly innovative in design, none of them ever experienced damage or loss of life because of a failure or defect in the nuclear power systems, for whose design, construction, and operation Admiral Rickover was responsible.

It should be obvious that my service on the *Pomfret* was what I consider to be ideal. In my own career, I have tried to conform my role as a leader to the standards of Captain Williams. It causes me concern that some of those who have worked for me see a closer likeness to Admiral Rickover. I recently overheard one of my associates remark, "When we make a decision to do something, we begin looking for a calendar. Jimmy looks at his watch." I can't deny that I am a demanding superior; my only explanation—not excuse—is that I try to equal the effort of those who work with me.

Whether within a church, among a crew of workers building a house, in a family, or in a nation, I have noticed that isolation comes with increasing power or prestige. This can breed arrogance, as truth and sharing suffer when others are not willing to speak up to us or to correct our errors. This is true in military organizations and in governments, including democracies like ours, except that in a free society even the top officials can expect criticism, both constructive and otherwise, from political adversaries and the news media. Appreciated or not, this provides a very beneficial self-corrective influence.

These restraints are not available within a dictatorship, where the leaders are surrounded by sycophants and never hear frank criticism or receive strong advice. The all-powerful shah of Iran was facing vocal but relatively peaceful opposition to some of his policies in 1977, when he came to visit me in Washington. He scoffed at my warnings about the excessively brutal reaction of his secret police, SAVAK, to some demonstrations in the city streets. The next year, after a full-fledged revolution erupted, one of his closest advisers came to the Oval Office to tell me that for several years the shah had completely isolated himself from anyone who might question his decisions. He would not even permit Iran's top commanders of the army, navy, and air force to consult with one another. The consequences are well known: Despite strong support from the

United States and other allies, in January 1979 the shah was forced to leave his country and live in exile until his death.

There are special scriptural admonitions concerning those who hold high public office, and I was reminded of them throughout my terms as governor and president. I remembered Paul's urging Timothy to pray for "kings, and for all that are in authority, that we may lead a quiet and peaceable life in all godliness and honesty" (1 Timothy 2:2). I realized that any moral responsibilities I had as a Christian were greatly magnified when millions of people could be affected by my actions and my example.

I enjoyed being president, but during that time I felt a special burden. The questions that had to be answered in the Oval Office were the most difficult ones our nation faced, those that could not be resolved in the offices of mayors or governors or in corporate boardrooms. Knowing how many lives could be affected by my decisions, I felt a special need for wisdom and a sense of God's presence. Although I had a lot of advice from all sides, it was a lonely job during times of crisis or when the issues were especially controversial.

I prayed more during those four years than at any other time in my life, just asking for God's guidance in making the right decisions on behalf of the American people. There was a small private office a few steps from the Oval Office where I kept my personal books, papers, photographs, and mementos. I would go back to this place for my most serious prayers. Also, I started each day by reciting one or two brief thoughts while walking past the Rose Garden on the way from our living quarters in the White House to my office. One of them was a verse from the Nineteenth Psalm: "Let the words of my mouth and the meditation of my heart be acceptable in Thy sight, O Lord, my strength and my redeemer." The effort to maintain a partnership with God was reassuring to me and, at the same time, a humbling experience, helping me in my effort to resist the temptations of isolation and arrogance that all leaders face.

   Some of the loneliest and most difficult decisions in government involve the use of military force. The president, as commander in chief, can cause or prevent the massive loss of human life.

   Nowadays, one of the most hotly debated historical questions is whether President Truman made the right decision in ordering the atomic bomb to be dropped on Hiroshima. I vividly remember sitting on the steel deck of an old battleship in the North Atlantic on August 5, 1945, assembled with all the crew to hear an important announcement from our commander in chief. The ship's loudspeaker system and the intervening wireless transmission made the president's flat Missouri voice seem even more surreal. The message itself was just as otherworldly. Truman had authorized the use of "an atomic bomb," a weapon of indescribable power, against Japan.

   All of us knew about the enormous casualties it had cost

the United States to take Okinawa from the sea. American troops had fought their way from landing ships to shore, and then foot by foot forward, from trench to trench and cave to cave, against ferocious opposition from the Japanese defenders. There were almost 50,000 U.S. casualties, with 12,000 dead. Ten times as many Japanese were killed, along with a third of the island's civilian population. Everyone in the military forces made mental projections about losses to be expected in an attempt to conquer the Japanese homeland. We heard estimates of up to a million American casualties, plus many more Japanese. Therefore, we were relieved and elated at the prospect of an early end of the war through a Japanese surrender. We all agreed that President Truman had made the right decision.

Now, more than fifty years later, that decision is still the subject of painful reappraisals. The horrors of a nuclear attack are being compared with what might have happened during weeks of massive bombing with conventional force, followed by the mainland invasion. In 1984, I was the first senior American statesman to visit Hiroshima, and I was deeply moved by the remaining evidence of destruction, and the estimates of 66,000 deaths from the attack. Clearly this was a devastating military blow with horrific human consequences.

Still, I believe that Truman's decision to use the bomb was correct. Remember, we were in a declared war, defending democracy, our nation, and our citizens. In wartime, a commander in chief cannot make protecting the enemy his preeminent concern; the lives of his own troops and citizens are more important. This is the nature of warfare.

Truman's decision has to be kept in perspective, not only about casualties that might have been avoided but about those experienced with the use of conventional weapons. In British raids on Hamburg, Germany, in July 1943, 50,000 civilians were killed; about 7 million perished in the German attacks on Stalingrad; and the total casualties of World War II were 55 million, 30 million of them civilians.

Although most Japanese strongly disagree, it seems to me that this difficult decision had two overriding benefits. Much greater invasion casualties were avoided, and the terrible evidence of atomic power has proved to be a major deterrent to its subsequent use. Thus, in the context of the vast, almost unimaginable evil of a world war, the lesser evil of using the first atomic weapon may have benefited humanity in the long run—though at an awful price.

Unlike some people of faith, I don't believe that pacifism is a necessary element of Christianity. This is a choice I made when I joined the navy. I knew there would be times, during war, when I might have to take human life in defense of my country. I accepted that. Had my Christianity been of the type that the Quakers and some others espouse, I would have been a conscientious objector rather than serve in the military. (I might also never have accepted political office, since this could have required me, as president, to send soldiers to their deaths.) But pacifism was not my choice.

Sacrificing lives in defense of our nation is sometimes necessary, and as a submarine office and then as commander in chief during the Cold War years, I was prepared to use the weapons at our disposal to destroy a Soviet submarine or respond to a nuclear missile or any other military attack that threatened our nation. This decision applied to a direct nuclear response against Soviet targets, most of which had been carefully designated since the administration of Dwight Eisenhower.

Even before my inauguration as president, I was thoroughly briefed about our military forces, and I consulted then and throughout my term with wise and knowledgeable people who shared my cautious approach to the use of our military power. My primary commitment was to protect America's interests while living peacefully with the Soviet Union. If peacekeeping efforts failed, as happened before World Wars I and II, I was prepared to use force if necessary. In addition, the mutual know-ledge of our mighty response capability was the greatest possible deterrence to an enemy attack and the destructiveness of the alternative—a third world war. Thus, although the life-and-death power I held as commander in chief was sobering, I was and am convinced of the moral rightness of maintaining America's military strength.

My ability to defend American interests without engulfing our nation or the world in war was most severely tested during my last fourteen months in office. First, Soviet troops invaded Afghanistan and threatened to move farther, into either Pakistan or Iran. This was the major

strategic problem for me, but there was a more highly pub-
licized and emotional crisis. In the aftermath of the revolution in Iran, Islamic forces led by the Ayatollah Khomeini
overthrew the shah. In November of 1979, Iranian militants invaded the U.S. embassy and seized sixty-six Americans as hostages. Our nation has seldom suffered such
anguish or uncertainty. I had few clear options during
those fourteen months. Because of the symbolic importance of our failure to bring the hostages home, the intense
interest among our own citizens and throughout the world,
and the lack of a clearly preferable response to the crisis,
this was the worst experience of my political life.

There was hardly a person in our country who had any
access to me or to the news media who didn't advocate
some response. Some quietly recommended that we
submit to Iranian blackmail by apologizing for our nation's
historic support for the now exiled shah. The Iranian
militants demanded that he be delivered to them for trial
and likely execution in Tehran. Much stronger voices
demanded that we launch a military attack against Iran.
These issues were hotly debated, both in the public
arena and among those who came to see me in the Oval
Office.

From the beginning of the crisis, I had two preeminent
goals: to protect the interests and honor of my country and
to bring all the hostages back home to safety and freedom.
I never deviated from these commitments. We seriously
considered military action, which would have been quite
popular and easy for me to order. However, I was con-

cerned that if I punished Iran in this way, the hostages would be brutalized or killed. Instead, I quickly sent the ayatollah an unpublicized warning, using multiple channels to be sure he received it. In essence, it said, "If you abuse a hostage, we will interrupt all trade between Iran and the outside world. If you kill one, we will respond militarily." In addition, I applied economic pressure by seizing more than $12 billion of Iranian deposits and urging our allies and supporters to refrain from trading with Iran.

Although a number of hostages were soon released, fifty-two were held captive throughout the balance of my term, an apparent reflection on my strength as a leader and, for many, on the power and prestige of the United States.

In April 1980, we made an unsuccessful effort to rescue the hostages. My orders were, if possible, to avoid any military confrontation or bloodshed, but eight Americans were killed in a tragic accident. Finally, through intense negotiations during the last three days and nights of my administration, during which time I never went to bed, we were able to achieve all our long-sought goals. At 10:00 A.M. on January 20, 1981, all the hostages were in a plane on the Tehran runway, waiting to leave Iran. The Ayatollah Khomeini finally permitted them to depart two hours later, a few minutes after my term ended, and two days later I met them when they arrived in Wiesbaden, Germany.

Not only did we secure the release of the hostages but

we retained enough Iranian assets to pay all claims by
Americans who had suffered financial losses as a result of
the Iranian revolution.

Although the hostage crisis was profoundly troubling, I
have faced different but equally difficult personal challenges, as have almost all other people. As mentioned in
this book, I have had to confront physical danger, financial
despair, family tragedy, political failure, and quandaries
concerning my career. In all such crises, self-analysis,
self-questioning, and prayer have been the heart of my
approach.

Prayer is the most essential element here. Even when I
was reluctant to share my problems and my unanswered
questions with any other human being, including Rosalynn, I was always able to share them with God. Prayer
helps me to analyze the problem I face and to understand
myself, including those things that are buried deep within
me. This opens up a very important healing process.
Unfortunately, the assurance my Christian faith promises
to me is a treasure I don't always tap. Sometimes I go a
long way down the road in a quandary, suffering inside,
before finally I ask myself, "Why don't I talk to God
about it?"

When I pray in such times, I try to ask myself three key
questions: Are the goals I am pursuing appropriate? Am I
doing the right thing, based on my personal moral code,
my Christian faith, and the duties of my current position?

And, finally, have I done my best, based on the alternatives open to me? If I present all these issues to God, and then make the best possible decisions I can, things often work out well. But if I've tried everything I can and still fail, I find that I can say, "So be it." Putting the problem in God's hands gives me a degree of peace that lets me live with the outcome, whatever it may be.

Not that this comes naturally to me. I return frequently to a favorite lesson from the Epistle of James: Adversity and failure can lead not to hopelessness or despair but to new opportunity, perhaps to the pursuit of new goals that God has in mind for us, which may be greater than those we set for ourselves. I can never be certain of the wisdom of my decisions, but reliance on my faith gives me a greater level of assurance and equanimity.

I have reconsidered my decisions as president many times since leaving office, and a number of books have been written about the Iranian revolution and the seizure of the hostages. I have no doubt that the fact that our diplomats were still being held on election day was the major factor in my failure to win another term, but I cannot think of anything I could have done differently that would have achieved the same successful result.

Sixteen years later, I remain convinced that the wisest course for a mighty nation when confronted with a challenge like the hostage crisis is one of caution and restraint. For a person of faith, in particular, I believe that all decisions of war and peace must be made with the awareness that human life is never to be lightly sacrificed. Although as president I was prepared to use our powerful force if necessary, I have always been thankful that, in concluding my presidential memoirs, I could quote Thomas Jefferson: "I have the consolation to reflect that during the period of my administration not a drop of the blood of a single citizen was shed by the sword of war."

To Establish Justice

M ost Americans are committed to do what is right and just, to be concerned about others, to be champions of peace, to bridge the chasm between ourselves and the needy, to alleviate their suffering, to keep our environment clean, and to try to comprehend and demonstrate that in God's sight others are as worthy as we are. These are moral, even spiritual commitments, yet Americans have historically used our social institutions—including government—for help in pursuing them. Despite the justifiable criticism of and sometimes disillusionment with political processes, it is often government, and not the Christian churches, that is in the forefront of the struggle to "bring good news to the poor, to proclaim freedom for the prisoners, recovery of sight for the blind, and to release the oppressed," to use the words of Jesus as he announced his own ministry (Luke 4:18).

As a Christian who has served our nation as a statesman and political leader, I've frequently pondered the relationship between religious beliefs and the duties of a citizen. One of my most challenging and enjoyable tasks is lecturing at Emory University. During my first year of teaching, I was asked to discuss my life as a politician and as a church member—to compare politics and religion, or churches and governments I have known.

It surprised my religion and theology students when I said that the majority of church members are more self-satisfied, more committed to the status quo, and more exclusive of nonsimilar people than are most political officeholders I have known. Some congregations are more like spectators than participants, depending on the pastor and a professional staff to provide the program. Officeholders must be involved in the action. In political arenas there is an inherent and unavoidable mechanism for public assessment of performance against a standard of excellence, a degree of rivalry in dealing with human problems in the most dedicated and effective manner, and severe consequences for those who are seen to fail.

Whether campaigning or serving in office, a politician cannot avoid the most difficult and controversial subjects. They are the ones on which the news reporters focus and on which judgments will be made on election day.

When I was serving on a county school board, in the

Georgia senate, in the governor's office, and in the White House, I spent a major portion of my time exploring how I might resolve the difficult issues. How could I join with others in feeding the hungry, clothing the naked, providing homes for the homeless, educating the illiterate, eliminating the stigma of poverty or racial discrimination, making peace and resolving differences between people, preventing crime, rehabilitating prisoners, and ensuring justice? These were not just occasional concerns but were constant preoccupations for me and for most others who served with me in political office.

The same degree of commitment and willingness to address the problems of society is rare in our religious congregations. I have been a member of some good churches, at home in Plains and near where we lived in Atlanta and Washington. Our men's classes have included some of the finest and most dedicated community leaders, and we have been proud in the practice of our Christian faith. It was common for us, as Thanksgiving or Christmas approached, to do something especially benevolent for the poor people near our place of worship. After we'd taken up a nice collection, a frequent remark was, "Why don't we call the welfare office and get the names and addresses of a few poor families, so we can take them what they need for a fine holiday meal?" But this was a special seasonal interest in the needy, not one that prevailed throughout the year.

Our governments are obviously fallible, and they deserve criticism for many defects and failures. Moral standards are often ignored or circumvented. There are embarrassing revelations of malfeasance among office-holders, and some of them have been convicted of crimes. But some of the same problems afflict the religious world.

It is interesting to compare the moral standards of government and religion. Without going into the more esoteric aspects of the question, let me make the point with a somewhat humorous example. When Rev. Pat Robertson announced his candidacy for president in 1988, he meticulously went down a long list of claims he had made as a religious leader and television evangelist and publicly corrected them as he prepared to enter the more demanding and carefully scrutinized world of politics.

At its highest, government aspires to embody and defend values that are shared with religion. The great twentieth-century theologian Reinhold Niebuhr said, "To establish justice in a sinful world is the whole sad duty of the political order. There has never been justice without law; and all laws are the stabilization of certain social equilibria, brought about by pressures and counter-pressures in society, and expressed in the structures of government" (*Reinhold Niebuhr on Politics*, p. 180). Niebuhr's point is that the highest possible goal of a government or a society is justice: to treat people fairly, to guarantee their individual rights, to guard against discrimination, to try to resolve arguments peacefully. That's beautiful, isn't it? That's what a government should do.

However, any government, even the most benevolent, has inherent limitations. The best it can do is strive to establish a society that enhances freedom, equality, and justice. There are deeper religious values, such as atonement, forgiveness, and love, that transcend what government can achieve. When governments reach their limits, the teachings of Jesus Christ and of the prophets of other faiths must prevail: "You shall love the Lord your God—and your neighbor as yourself." We have a much greater opportunity beyond government to have our hearts united, to reach out personally to those in need, and to expand our lives in demonstrating self-sacrificing love, love for the unlovable.

There have been times when government was generally trusted to stand for some of the transcendent values that represent the best in humankind. Today, however, American attitudes toward government seem to be dominated by cynicism and pessimism. Tragically, American governments at all levels are seen to have gotten away from the concepts of forgiveness and reconciliation. Our society is steadily growing more racially and economically polarized. One reason is that many poor and minority Americans are convinced, with good reason, that the basic system of justice and law enforcement is not fair.

Though this problem is becoming increasingly serious, it is not new. When my three sons were in college, I realized that they might be experimenting with marijuana. This was of concern to me, but I was confident that an arrest would not destroy their lives. Ours was a prominent family, and I knew the sheriff and judge well. I always felt that they would not want to send "one of the Carter boys" to the state penitentiary. My promise to enroll them in a military school or to guarantee their future actions most likely would have substituted for prison. I also realized, at least subliminally, that if arrested on the same charge, our poor and noninfluential neighbors would not have fared so well.

This was the same era when the most distinguished lawyers (including a majority of U.S. Supreme Court justices) maintained that "separate but equal" should be the law of the land. Many white church leaders "proved," through selected Bible verses, that God had ordained the superiority of whites.

In attempting to control crime, there has been an alternating emphasis on rehabilitation and punishment. During the early 1970s, reacting against the ravages of racial segregation, there was a common desire, even competition, among us state governors to reform injustices in the penal system. In 1971, as a new governor, I visited the penitentiaries with Georgia's enlightened prison director, Dr. Ellis MacDougall, and met with the incarcerated men and women. We found abominable conditions, with some prisoners having been in solitary confinement for more than five years. Almost invariably, the inmates were relatively defenseless, disproportionately poor and black, and 35 percent of them were mentally retarded.

We uncovered many cases of convictions on false accusations, trials with inadequate or nonexistent legal counsel, and confessions obtained under duress or with false promises of leniency. There was an unwholesome traffic in pardons and paroles by some lawyers, even by state legislators who had no legal training. They would charge relatively ignorant family members exorbitant monthly fees in return for helping to obtain what were actually routine paroles of penitentiary inmates.

When the laws are written and administered by the most powerful leaders in a society, it is human nature for them to understand, justify, and protect the interests of themselves and people like them. Many injustices arise from this natural human failing. In a Law Day speech as governor, I delineated some of these abuses to startled alumni of the University of Georgia Law School. My son, Jack, a law school student, was in the audience, and later I wrote a poem about the disagreement we had on this topic.

To a Young Lawyer, My Son

One day I lashed out at my lawyer friends,
and you were there
to hear me ask why legal ways are often
so unfair;
why, instead of what is just and right,
time and again
money, shrewd delays, and courtroom skills
seem to win.
I listened later to your angry claim
that you, with your
more legal mind, could understand their needs
and do much more
than I to help the cheerless poor and weak,
who rarely can
rely on laws designed by us to keep
the power in hand.
The problem's not that on the law we have
a different view—

it's how to shield our way of life, and share
with others too.

In Georgia, we established early release and work
release programs. I personally recruited and helped train
volunteer probation officers, who were Lions, Rotarians,
Kiwanians, and members of other service organizations.
We established a program of giving thorough examinations
to all incoming inmates to determine their existing and
potential skills, and helped them plan their careers for the
years in prison and after release.

Many governors embraced this approach, and it
resulted in a substantial decrease in the number of prisoners. My own experience in Georgia was that recidivism
was reduced. Records show that a 9 percent *annual* increase
in the U.S. prison population since 1980 has paralleled a
dramatic 48 percent increase in violent crime from 1979 to
1992. Clearly, filling the prisons has not reduced crime as
promised.

In 1977, the U.S. Supreme Court ended a thirteen-year
prohibition on the death penalty. There is no proof that
capital punishment deters capital crimes; in fact, statistics
indicate just the opposite. In California, for instance, there
was a 4.8 percent annual increase in murders before this
ruling. With more than six executions per year during the
next decade and a half, the murder rate increased 10.0 percent annually. There are now more than 3,000 Americans
on death row, almost all of them poor, often mentally
retarded, and disproportionately African-American. It is

sobering to know that 50 have been freed since 1976 because they were proven innocent after having been sentenced to die. The days of prison reform and rehabilitation of inmates are gone. One of the most effective campaign themes among political demagogues today is the harshness of their treatment of offenders. It is more popular for a governor to boast of building prison cells than schoolrooms. The range of capital crimes has skyrocketed at the state and federal level, and death penalties are executed with a literal vengeance. America now has more than 1 million prison inmates, a higher proportion of citizens incarcerated than any other industrialized country on earth. (Russia ranks second to us.)

One of the most dramatic changes, initiated in California, is the "three strikes and you're out" sentencing requirement, which eliminates any possibility of freedom for a repeat felon. The government of my own state, Georgia, trumped this by imposing "*two* strikes and you're out," and the governor is now attempting to limit physical exercise, library use, and similar "privileges" for inmates. Once again, shackled prisoners are working along the roads in Alabama, and visitors who come to enjoy the sight can buy "chain gang" hats and other souvenirs.

These changes have been made because harsh treatment is popular with voters, but there is no evidence that it deters crime. With little chance for rehabilitation, hopelessness prevails in prisons, where, early in 1996, the rising sense of injustice and despair led to an epidemic of revolts.

As these data show, the choices made by our leaders in

government can have a profound effect on the social and spiritual well-being of millions of citizens. In political life, the principles I followed were established partially in laws, partially in the general platform of the Democratic party, and partially through my personal interests and commitments. They involved such hotly debated issues as environmental quality, affirmative action, the nature of the tax system, a general support for workers' rights versus those of big business, and a concern for the poor and elderly. I also believed in a strong defense system, minimal deficits, and maximum transfer of authority from the federal government to local officials and individuals. Although something of a mixed bag, the array of platform commitments I made was fairly complete, and extrapolating from them helped me decide how to address unexpected issues. The values embodied in my political positions spelled out, in effect, how I defined *justice* and chose to strive for it as governor and president.

There is never hope of infallibility, because the future can't be predicted accurately, and there are always arguments, even among leaders in the same party, concerning the application of general principles to specific questions or local communities. In no case is it possible to embody the pure ideals of justice in a system of laws. This is what Reinhold Niebuhr meant by justice as the highest *goal* of a group, a society, or a government. His definition of justice is quite complicated, requiring many pages to express. However, in brief, it involves the proper juxtaposition of order, equality, and freedom. A just system of government must be designed to arbitrate and adjudicate competing claims and conflicting rights.

The Bible is ambiguous concerning our duties in regard to secular authority. Paul told the Romans, "Let every person be subject to the governing authorities ... those who resist will incur judgment" (Romans 13:1–2). But the Hebrew prophets did not hesitate to denounce those in power when they did not act justly in the eyes of God. Their demand, in the words of Amos, was that rulers should "Let justice roll down like waters, and righteousness like an everflowing stream" (Amos 5:24). When justice is denied because of unfair laws or misguided or corrupt leaders, it is our duty as citizens to struggle for changes in the laws and the system that enforces them. But what should we do, as people of faith, when the laws support acts that are evil according to the religious values we hold? Jesus, Paul, and the disciples all gave the answer to this question. Civil disobedience is in order when human laws are contrary to God's commands to us. Jesus went to his death and Paul spent his final years in prison rather than conform to religious and secular laws which they could not accept. In our own century, civil rights activists in America and Mahatma Gandhi in India demonstrated the necessity and effectiveness of such action.

We are not required to submit to the domination of authority without assessing whether it is contrary to our faith or our beliefs. Even in a democracy like ours, each of us must confront and examine our national policies. When I was in the White House, I disagreed with some of the laws I was sworn to enforce, such as those concerning energy, the environment, and abortion, and I attempted in every legitimate way to change or minimize what I considered to be their adverse effect.

When governments fail to defend real justice in Niebuhr's sense, it is a duty for citizens informed by religious faith and a sense of morality to challenge the powerful and demand change. In the 1960s, when my sons were of college age, the young people used peaceful demonstrations and other forms of protest to change American policies in three of the most important issues that faced our government: civil rights, the environment, and the Vietnam War. Civil disobedience, of course, includes a willingness to accept the penalty for breaking the law one opposes. Later, in the 1980s, our daughter, Amy, was arrested on three occasions for participating in student demonstrations against apartheid in South Africa and once for condemning the policies of the CIA during the Contra war in Nicaragua.

Gandhi, Martin Luther King, Jr., and the biblical heroes made it clear that nonviolence and tolerance are the necessary hallmarks of effective civil disobedience. Understood in this way, this action is the prerogative of any private citizen.

A notably successful mixture of religion and politics was the civil rights crusade of the 1950s and 1960s. The segregation and abuse of African-Americans was a gross violation of both the spirit of our Constitution and the basic teachings of Jesus. The movement led by Dr. Martin Luther King, Jr., in the black churches and such organizations as the National Association for the Advancement of Colored People and the Congress of Racial Equality was watched closely by Southern segregationists, who soon judged them not likely to succeed in breaking down racial barriers.

However, a radical change occurred when the young black and white civil rights activists of the Student Nonviolent Coordinating Committee began sitting down at white-only lunch counters, daring to disrupt normal commercial and legal proceedings. They aroused even more concern and condemnation when they attempted to enter church sanctuaries in order to worship with white Christians.

Those forces merged, slowly and inexorably, always with the core of their support and their major forum in the black religious congregations. It was this full coalition, and ultimately the politicians and federal courts, that broke down the racial barriers of our segregated society—most often with white congregations opposing the change. Despite setbacks, arrests, and physical abuse, the leaders were inspired and strengthened by the conviction that their cause was just and that God was with them. Their adoption of peace, nonviolence, and the symbols and trappings of religion in their rallies, sermons, and songs shook the convictions of white Christians who believed that segregation was compatible with biblical teachings. I saw this within my own church and community.

Many white Americans in all regions during slavery and

segregation times were willing to accept these evils without questioning them, and many of our black neighbors were reluctant to challenge the racist system. Its violation of basic religious values seems clear now, but, during the era of "separate but equal" laws, it was the way of life for us. When civil rights emerged in the early 1950s as a major political issue, respected religious leaders were invited to speak to the members of our Plains Baptist brotherhood. Most of our church leaders nodded approvingly while, with carefully selected verses, the speakers "proved" that segregation was condoned or even mandated by God. Their reassuring testimony was corroborated by our nation's distinguished "constitutional lawyers," including Supreme Court justices, who maintained that racial segregation was acceptable under the U.S. Constitution.

Even during these times, however, there was an evolutionary, unpublicized conversion of most white Southerners by the civil rights leaders concerning the compatibility of their cause with the teachings of Jesus. But this was a slow process. When the issue of accepting black worshipers was addressed by our congregation in Plains in 1963, I spoke in favor of welcoming them and any others who came in good faith. We usually had about fifty members attend our monthly conferences, but on this occasion every pew was filled. When a vote was taken, only one other person voted with our family to admit everyone, while fifty opposed the motion. The significant thing was that almost two hundred others abstained.

A year later, in 1964, the Georgia legislature voted on the Twenty-fourth Amendment to the U.S. Constitution, which prohibited poll taxes as a prerequisite to voting. Although we no longer collected such taxes in our state, this amendment was considered an important civil rights proposal, since poll taxes were still used in some states to prevent voting by black citizens. Formerly in Georgia and then in other states, the tax had been allowed to accumulate each year, beginning at age twenty-one, so that a payment exceeding forty-five dollars was required to permit some older people to cast a ballot. When we were debating this issue, I received my only telephone calls from Georgia's congressional leaders in Washington, urging me and other state senators to oppose the measure. Despite these efforts, we voted overwhelmingly to ratify the amendment.

It is well known that during segregation days many white Southerners respected and often loved individual Negroes who were our neighbors. We didn't have to introduce ourselves to our black friends when legal integration came. Nowadays, secular life in most schools, businesses, and governments is legally integrated. Maranatha Baptist Church warmly welcomes all visitors who come to attend our services, and we are proud of a few interracial worship events in Plains, such as joint choir services on Easter.

Even when they are welcomed in our own and other predominantly white churches, however, few black Christians choose to join these congregations. They may feel that the welcome is not genuine; there are ties to family and friends that are binding on Sundays; or it may be that our rigid two-hour periods for both Sunday school and a sermon, ending at noon, are not attractive to worshipers accustomed to a more leisurely and unstructured session that often extends far into the afternoon.

Unfortunately, all too few congregations make an enthusiastic and effective effort to break down the racial and social barriers that still divide us. One of the finest programs to pursue this goal is Habitat for Humanity, a Christian-based organization that builds homes in partnership with homeless families or those living in substandard housing. Although the primary purpose of Habitat is to improve the lives of needy families by providing them with shelter and the dignity of decent housing, an equal benefit is to bring together people from widely differing backgrounds who might otherwise never meet, enriching us all with a reminder of our common humanity.

Not everyone understands this. When Habitat began serving poor families in our county, one of the wealthiest local women called Millard Fuller, the founder. "Why don't you build a house for my maid?" she demanded angrily. "She needs a new home as much as anyone." Millard explained the criteria for choosing homeowners, pulled out a standard form, and began to ask a few questions.

"How long has she worked for you?"

"Twenty-three years."

"Is she a good and reliable worker?"

"Of course. She comes every day, without fail."

"What is her name?"

"I don't know her last name, but her first one is Maude."

Like Maude's employer, many of us do not know or really care about our next-door neighbors. One obstacle to breaking down racial barriers is that we don't quite know what to do. How many of us actually know a poor family well enough to have a cup of coffee in their living room or kitchen? Or know the names of their teenage sons? Or take their kids to a movie or baseball game with our children? Or, God forbid, invite them to our house?

Those of us who have everything we need and, in general, make all the decisions about our society simply do not know those who are living in poverty, alienation, and despair. The families who find it difficult to get good jobs, decent homes, safe neighborhoods, and good medical care and education do not know or trust their privileged neighbors, the court system, or the police to care about their plight. The prisoners, drug addicts, alcoholics, homeless, teenage mothers, and school dropouts have little hope or confidence in the system. I think this incompatibility between the rich and powerful and the poor and weak is the root cause of the worst problems our country faces.

In announcing his ministry, Jesus spoke to this very point: "The Spirit of the Lord is on me, because he has anointed me to preach good news to the poor. He has sent me to proclaim freedom for the prisoners and recovery of sight for the blind, to release the oppressed" (Luke 4:18). He went on for three years to fulfill this commitment—and to give Christians the same goals.

As president, I tried to make human rights a core value of my administration. This emphasis was derived from my experience growing up in the South, and from the guilt I shared with others over the way we deprived our black neighbors of their human rights. I find it incredible to recall the social customs we took for granted in the South in decades past. I now ask, as almost all white Southerners do, "How could this have been? Why did we not see that racial segregation was a millstone around our necks as well as those of our black neighbors? How could we reconcile the way we acted with the teachings of Jesus Christ?" By the time I was elected president, most Southerners saw the evil of this very clearly.

My concern about relations between the races was based on a lifetime of experience and was more a personal commitment than a political stance. But I had also accumulated a broad base of support among black Georgians while I was governor, and they participated fully in my presidential campaign. Early in 1976, then-Congressman Andrew Young took me to meet with the members of the Congressional Black Caucus. The other Democratic presidential candidates were better known in Washington than I was; I'd only met two of the two dozen or so black congressmen.

Andy reported that all the candidates who'd previously met with the group had seemed ill at ease and had been quick to agree with virtually every policy suggestion the caucus members made. At the end of each meeting, there was a final, routine question: How many black people do you have on your campaign staff? Most of them had one or two, and one had three. The most politically liberal of the candidates replied that he was currently interviewing people in hopes of hiring one.

When it was my turn to meet with the caucus, I felt at

home, and I was not reluctant to disagree with many things they said about mandatory quotas, costly social programs, and other topics. It was a frank and unrestrained discussion of some major political issues. But when they asked me, "How many blacks do you have on your campaign staff?" I didn't have the slightest idea. So I started naming them aloud to count them up, and when I was finished, I realized that I had twenty-two. I left the room while Andy Young stayed behind, and he later told me that, although I'd disagreed with the congressmen on most issues, there was a positive attitude toward me in the room. With the strong support of Andy, Martin Luther King, Sr., and many other black leaders who knew me personally, I later received 85 percent of the black vote.

I have often been asked if there were many serious conflicts between my religious beliefs and my duties as an elected official. There were very few occasions when I felt torn between my own faith and my obligation to comply with my oath to "preserve, protect, and defend the Constitution of the United States." There is probably not a great incompatibility between our patriotic ideals for America and Judeo-Christian values. Justice, equal opportunity, human rights, freedom, democracy, truth—those are the kinds of things that were spelled out by Thomas Jefferson and others in the founding days of our country, and we still would like to preserve them.

However, there were some harshly debated interpretations of the law that confronted me with difficult choices. I was thankful that there were no executions of criminals while I was governor or president. One of my fundamental political beliefs is that we should avoid modifying the Constitution in response to cyclical changes in American public opinion. Therefore, I opposed constitutional amendments that would have permitted mandatory prayer in public schools or totally prohibited abortions. However, the latter issue was one over which I had great concern. I have never been able to believe that Jesus would have approved the taking of a human life, but the difficult question then remained: When does a fetus become a human being? My duty was to comply with the rulings of the Supreme Court, but I did everything possible to minimize the need for and attractiveness of abortions.

Some of the simple parables of Jesus have to be interpreted flexibly to fit complex and unpredictable situations. One of these is his use of a Roman coin to draw a line between secular and religious authorities: "Render to Caesar the things that are Caesar's and to God the things that are God's" (Mark 12:17). My father interpreted this counsel strictly and extended it to the premise that the government should not be involved either in religion or in his personal affairs. Although Georgia overwhelmingly supported the three reelections of President Franklin Roosevelt, Daddy never supported him after 1935, when a New Deal program required farmers to plow up knee-high cotton and kill young pigs in order to lower production and increase prices.

I inherited my own support for the separation of church

and state from my father, I guess, but I came to realize while holding public office how ambiguous is the line between the secular and the sacred.

I know from sad experience the dangers of mixing my religious faith with my political career. An attempt to explain my religious beliefs to a large audience almost prevented my becoming president. This is one of the best-known events in U.S. political history, but until now I have tried to explain it only in my Sunday school classes.

During the late summer of 1976, I was far ahead of President Gerald Ford in public opinion polls and holding a steady lead. Wanting as much publicity as possible, and particularly interested in attracting support from young voters, my overconfident staff and I agreed to the entreaties of *Playboy* magazine to do a series of short interviews, mostly while flying from one campaign stop to another, that would become a definitive cover story. We insisted that the final text of the article be submitted to my press secretary for editing, at least for accuracy, before it could be published. The *Playboy* editors agreed, but I still answered their questions carefully with everything recorded on tape.

The final interview was in the living room of my home, and it went well. The reporter thanked me and turned off his tape recorder, and we moved to the front door to say good-bye. He said, apparently off the record, "Governor, there is still one thing that really concerns me. You are a farmer, living in a small town, who has pledged never to lie to the American people. You also claim to be a born-again Christian. The citizens of our country and other public officials are not perfect. How will you be able to relate to them, when you consider yourself to be so much better than they are?"

This took me aback, and I tried to describe my real feelings. I explained that Jesus was particularly concerned with human pride and a sense of superiority over others, and condemned those who judged others. I then moved to the Sermon on the Mount, in an attempt to explain further. If you hate your brother, the sin is like murder. It is necessary to love your enemies, not just your friends. Public prayer is its own reward. You should fast and give alms in secret. And then I quoted the crucial words of Jesus: "You have heard that it was said, 'You shall not commit adultery'; but I say to you, that everyone who looks on a woman to lust for her has committed adultery with her already in his heart" (Matthew 5:27–28).

The reporter asked me if I had ever been guilty of adultery, and his next question was predictable. I replied truthfully, "Yes, I have lusted. . . ."

The reporter left, and I felt quite pleased with the entire interview, not realizing that he had surreptitiously restarted the tape recorder as we stood at the door. What he had recorded was too good to be submitted for our review.

Several weeks later, while I was emulating Harry Truman on a whistle-stop railway campaign across Pennsylvania, I found that dozens of reporters on the train were absorbed with the new issue of *Playboy*. To my amazement,

I was besieged with questions about my sex life. At first I thought this was just a passing joke, but I was wrong. It became the dominant news story of my candidacy, and my popularity dropped precipitously. Any attempts to explain the Christian theology behind my answers only served to keep the issue alive. Reporters became instant students of religion and rushed to interview famous pastors and television evangelists. Almost all of them denied fervently that they had ever had sexual thoughts in their minds or hearts—except, of course, for their wives.

Rosalynn has always told me that she saw this as merely another unpredictable political crisis that would have to be faced and overcome. When asked by reporters for her reaction, she responded that she was certain of my love, that she was familiar with the Bible verses and understood my explanation of them. My three sons, all in their twenties, were particularly angry at the preachers who professed their total innocence. Most of my campaign workers were distressed that we had made such a foolish mistake. I guess all of us felt that way. I was finally elected, but only by a narrow margin.

Having attained the White House, Rosalynn and I faced a different set of issues regarding our faith.

We had observed that my predecessors had invited Billy Graham and other famous preachers to conduct well-publicized worship services in the White House. We respected their right to do so, but we felt that for us to do the same would violate our concept of the church and state being kept separate. At the same time, we didn't want to let holding political office prevent our worshiping as normally as possible.

After I was elected governor, Rosalynn and I had visited a friend who was dying with cancer and had assured her that we intended to continue as members of the Baptist church congregation in Plains. We thought our friend would be pleased, but she immediately replied, "My mama always said that when you move your cookstove, you should move your church membership." Because of this remark, we became active members of the Baptist church nearest the governor's mansion in Atlanta and, later, the White House in Washington. I was a deacon in Atlanta's Northside Drive Baptist Church while governor, and I taught Sunday school several times a year at First Baptist Church while we were in Washington.

Whenever possible, Rosalynn and I went to Camp David for the weekends, and we were able to worship there in almost complete privacy. Our Sunday services were conducted by a chaplain from a nearby army base, early enough in the morning for him to return for his regular sermon to his troops. A few of our staff members and some of the navy personnel stationed there would attend with us, in a room set aside for this purpose. In 1978, during the thirteen days of Camp David negotiations between Israel and Egypt, we were able to convert the same little room each weekend to accommodate the religious services of the Jews, the Muslims, and the Christians. Now a chapel has been built on the grounds, with donations received while President Ronald Reagan was in office.

* * *

Americans are rightly sensitive about clashes between church and state, but conflicts between religion and government are not the only questions. There is also the issue of too much melding of the two. In Norway and Finland, for instance, a fixed portion of the taxes collected by the federal government goes to support the religious programs of officially accepted churches. There is debate among Christians in those countries about whether this is good or bad. We always have to struggle in our own Baptist church to meet our budget, so we can expand our church if our congregation grows, support our missionary family in Togo, give our preacher an adequate salary, and do other desirable things. To varying degrees, of course, all members feel that we have a direct involvement in the character and actions of the entire congregation. Being called upon for financial support is part of this involvement. I believe that forgoing our own financial responsibility and depending on government support would sap the vigor of the church.

Separation of church and state doesn't just protect religion from government meddling. It is also a positive good, encouraging Americans to support hundreds of varied and active religious denominations, worshiping God in churches, synagogues, mosques, and temples of every size and type.

How can diversity among sincere religious beliefs be a powerful unifying influence among us? Historically, this is not a strange concept. The signers of the Declaration of

Independence said that our people had the right "to assume among the Powers of the Earth the separate and equal Station to which the Laws of Nature and of Nature's God entitle them." They went on to remind the world that the people were "endowed by their Creator with certain unalienable Rights." In closing, they wrote, "And for the support of this declaration, with a firm Reliance on the Protection of Divine Providence, we mutually pledge to each other our lives, our Fortunes, and our sacred Honor." Thus, despite their varied faiths—Puritans, Quakers, Catholics, Baptists, and Deists—our founders joined together in invoking the aid of one creator and the shared values they derived from their belief in God.

However, to be certain that references to God, Creator, and Divine Providence did not imply any encroachment by a powerful government on religious freedom, the First Amendment of the Constitution stated clearly, "Congress shall make no law respecting an establishment of religion, or prohibiting the free exercise thereof." This was a burning issue among our nation's founders, since so many American families had come to this continent to escape religious persecution and to worship freely. For more than 200 years, the church-state relationship has been debated, but our Constitution has prevailed.

The fact is that the basic political principles of America are compatible with our deepest religious beliefs. With the exception of atheists, Jehovah's Witnesses, and a few others whose consciences do not permit it, we citizens can address our flag and pledge allegiance without qualms to "one nation, under God."

I grew up in a community that was racially, economically, and socially diverse. However, all of us—black and white, rich and poor, merchants and farmers—were Protestant Christians, and Democrats. It was only later, as a naval officer, governor, and president, that I had the responsibility of respecting the different religious faiths—and political beliefs—of others. World history has taught us that it is not easy for authoritarian leaders with deep religious beliefs to be tolerant of the divergent views of others.

It is obvious that the ways Americans deal with some of these issues have evolved with the passage of time. When I grew up in Plains, for instance, we had mandatory chapel every morning in school. We sang religious songs, had prayer, and recited memorized Bible verses. This can be justified in retrospect by the fact that we all shared the same faith. But nowadays, even if we have an overwhelming majority of Protestants but just a few Catholics, Jews, Muslims, or atheists in the classroom, it would not be proper for a teacher to force all the kids to worship the same way, or at all.

Even then, we were living in a changing world, and we had to accommodate evolving customs and standards, including different interpretations of the Scriptures and how rigidly they were to be observed. It was a surprise to me to learn that, before World War I, the running of trains was restricted in the United States on Sundays. Until after the Second World War, there were no baseball games played on Sunday, and I remember the blue law debate when I was in the Georgia Senate, which finally resulted in stores being legally open throughout the weekend.

There has been a metamorphosis in our lifestyles, and it continues at an ever more rapid pace. How can we deal with it successfully? The best advice I've ever known came from my former teacher Miss Julia Coleman, whom I quoted in my presidential inaugural address: "We must adjust to changing times and still hold to unchanging principles." For her, changing times meant the advent of gramophones, school buses, electricity, talking movies, and radio programs. For us, it means supersonic jets, genetic engineering, personal computers, and the Internet. Yet Miss Coleman's wisdom still holds true.

Searching for Peace

After I was defeated for reelection in 1980, it was a real temptation for Rosalynn and me simply to stay close to our home in Plains and care for our farmland. But we decided instead to embark on a new career. We wanted my presidential library to be more than just a repository for my official records, so we began plans for The Carter Center, an international peacemaking organization to be headquartered in Atlanta.

Our early vision of The Carter Center was just a vague hope that we could combine our secular and religious interests in worthwhile projects. At the time, I was still deeply concerned about the Middle East peace process, which my administration had helped begin at Camp David, and frustrated that the effort to follow up with the Palestinians, Jordan, and Syria had been largely abandoned by the Reagan administration. My hope was that, in some way, I could use my knowledge and experience in addressing this and other conflicts in the world and, with approval from Washington, perhaps Rosalynn and I could become involved in some mediation efforts. In the early 1980s, our visits to the Middle East were officially encouraged, and I always gave full reports to the secretary of state and the White House. On occasion, I would also meet secretly with Palestinian leaders.

I soon began to realize that there were many needs other than peacemaking that could not be met by the U.S. government or other official agencies. Increasingly, our center became a neutral forum within which diverse and even hostile groups could meet to explore common approaches to problems.

Since then, the scope of our interests has continued to expand, and we now see the inseparability of peace, justice, freedom, democracy, human rights, environmental protection, and the alleviation of physical suffering. Our work is almost entirely among the poorest and most needy people, in this country and in many foreign nations. In every Carter Center program, Rosalynn is a full partner with me, and she has been in charge of our efforts in the field of mental health. Under her leadership, more than sixty formerly uncooperative organizations now come together annually to share their common ideas and goals.

When we decided to establish The Carter Center, we sought help and advice from many sources. I visited more than fifty benevolent foundations, occasionally receiving financial support and always benefiting from information about needs we might fill that other organizations were not addressing. We also brought in former associates from my administration, experts from Harvard and George Mason Universities, and peacekeepers from the United Nations to give us advice on mediation techniques and ways of learning about the many relatively unpublicized conflicts in the world.

We wanted to involve the faith communities in some of our causes, and we assembled leaders from different religious groups to discuss how our center might serve them and act as a catalyst to expand our combined work. At one large meeting, we hosted representatives from about twenty Christian denominations, plus groups of Jews, Muslims, Hindus, Buddhists, Baha'is, and members of other faiths. Despite the many differences among us, there were two issues on which we could all agree: one was peace, and the other was the prevention and alleviation of suffering. From this has grown our Interfaith Health Program, within which many faith groups now share ideas and experiences through regional meetings, periodicals, and World Wide Web pages on the Internet.

The Carter Center has been operating in an especially interesting and important time on the international scene. With the end of the Cold War, we in the United States no longer face intense competition with a powerful Soviet Union for hegemony or influence in almost every region of the world. There is a void in international leadership, which offers us a comparatively blank slate on which to imprint the finest aspects of our nation's ideals. As a Christian, I think we can prove that it is possible to support the religious or spiritual values of compassion, sharing, and peace along with the democratic principles of freedom, equality, human rights, and self-rule.

When given the opportunity, though, our country has not always chosen to adopt the option of peace. During the last few years, the United States has been involved in many wars, one way or another. We gave at least tacit approval to Israel's disastrous invasion of Lebanon in 1982, then sent in U.S. Marines and bombed and strafed the villages around Beirut. We invaded and defeated Grenada. We invaded and destroyed a good portion of Panama. And on a more massive scale, we orchestrated the Persian Gulf War. In none of these cases did we first exhaust the opportunities for peaceful resolution of the dispute.

We Americans are proud of our military achievements, and war almost invariably brings instant popularity to the president, who changes in the public perception from a beleaguered civilian administrator to a dynamic commander in chief when our brave young men and women go into combat.

Yet with a deep and consistent commitment to peace, a powerful and admired America could have a tremendously beneficial influence on troubled regions of the world and could help both to resolve and to prevent needless wars. Many political (but not necessarily military) leaders disagree with these ideas and consider them weak, naïve, and overly idealistic. But in our work for The Carter Center, we witness firsthand the eagerness of people in war-torn or suffering nations for the peaceful interposition of American power. Such involvement would often be unsuccessful and frustrating, at times even politically unpopular. But peace efforts are closely related to all our ideals and moral values: human rights, freedom, democracy, and the alleviation of human suffering. Even when such efforts end in failure, they can greatly improve the reputation and influence of our country in areas of the world that do not share our own high opinion of America.

For some reason, Americans tend to see conflicts in terms of friend/enemy, angel/devil. This view is one of the major impediments to realizing our global potential as a champion of peace.

Consider a few well-known names on the international scene, including Anwar Sadat, Yasir Arafat, Kim Il Sung, Emile Jonassaint, Fidel Castro, and Hafiz al-Assad. These are, or were, all powerful, famous, nondemocratic rulers. Their names are "foreign," not Anglo-Saxon. All these men have at times been misunderstood, ridiculed, and totally condemned by the American public, and some of them deserve it. But like it or not, someone must be willing to deal with these kinds of leaders if we are to avert future wars and human suffering.

Most Americans now think of Egypt's Anwar Sadat quite favorably, but I remember that when he visited us in the White House for the first time in 1977, the vast majority of Americans looked upon almost all Arabs, including the Egyptian president, with great suspicion or animosity. Later, with his historic visit to Jerusalem, his agreement to the Camp David Accords, and the treaty with

Israel, he became a heroic peacemaker—and finally a
martyr to peace.

All too often, conflicts and wars arise when we fail to
consider the views of others or to communicate with them
about differences between us.

In my personal life, I sometimes find it difficult to
understand those with whom I disagree or those who con-
tradict me. Strangely, I find it easier to put myself in the
position of an adversary when I am involved in negotiations as a mediator or even as an antagonist. It seems
natural in those circumstances for me to attune my mind
away from myself and to a more objective point of view. As
president during the intense days of the Cold War, for
instance, I would sit in the Oval Office, glance at a big
globe, and try to view the world as Soviet President Leonid
Brezhnev did—living in a closed society, surrounded by
frozen seas, powerfully armed enemies, and doubtful allies.
The insights gained from this reflection helped me in
negotiating, when I tried to alleviate his concerns while
still pursuing the goals of my own country.

I used to argue vociferously with the Russian leaders
about human rights. It was disturbing for me, as president,
to hear Andrei Gromyko, the foreign minister of the Soviet
Union, say, "We don't have any human rights violations in
our country. Everybody in the Soviet Union has a place to
sleep, adequate medical care, and a job." I couldn't argue
when he quoted our own statistics about the number of

Americans who were homeless, lacked adequate health care, or were unemployed. Gromyko's argument was that these were examples of our failure to recognize our citizens' human rights.

Obviously, the Soviet citizens were assigned jobs, they had to live where they were told, and they didn't have the right to voice their opinions, choose their own leaders, avoid summary convictions and punishment, move to another country, or even know the facts about their own society or the outside world. These are gross violations of human rights as Americans define them. But it was not easy for either Gromyko or me to accept an expanded definition of human rights. We each had a convenient definition, one that caused us few twinges of conscience. Differences like these must be recognized and understood when negotiating with adversaries—without abandoning our own beliefs and principles.

Over the past fifteen years, we at The Carter Center have adopted a number of principles for making and keeping peace within and between nations. One of the most basic is that in political, military, moral, and spiritual confrontations, there should be an honest attempt at the reconciliation of differences before resorting to combat. The fact is that in most cases—though not all—there is enough common ground between adversaries to avoid violence and to permit people to live as neighbors, even if their differences are not resolved. However, there must be a basic desire for peace, enough respect for opponents to communicate with them, a willingness to reexamine one's own beliefs, and the personal and political courage to employ the principles of dispute resolution.

Provided I can obtain permission from our top government officials and believe that my efforts might be helpful, I feel no reluctance about having personal contact with people who have been branded as oppressive, dishonest, or even guilty of launching wars of aggression.

A typical but troubling example of these experiences came when I was asked by the International Red Cross and the UN High Commissioner for Refugees to help resolve a problem with the Ethiopian communist dictator, President Mengistu Haile Mariam. Tens of thousands of Somalian and Sudanese refugees had filled camps in Ethiopia, and the relief agencies reported that Mengistu was not permitting them to deliver food, water, and medicine. Since I was already in East Africa on Carter Center projects, I traveled to Addis Ababa, the capital of Ethiopia. At the time, the United States rightly had withdrawn its ambassador from the country in protest against the government's policies.

Mengistu welcomed Rosalynn and me to Addis and invited us to stay at the palace of the late emperor Haile Selassie. (It was generally believed that the eighty-three-year-old emperor had been smothered in bed by Mengistu's revolutionary forces in 1975.) So far as we knew, no American officials had ever visited Mengistu, but we found him to be frank with us and apparently willing to resolve the impasse with the international organizations. Through an interpreter, he explained that he was quite willing to see supplies go to the refugees but that the agencies had refused to permit deliveries by Ethiopians. It took only a brief discussion for him to accept our suggestion that his troops carry the supplies but that representatives of the international agencies monitor the procedure. This solution proved acceptable to all parties.

While there, I also suggested that peace talks be commenced between the Ethiopian government and their chief adversaries, revolutionaries from Eritrea and Tigre, in a war that had lasted more than two decades and caused more than a million deaths. Mengistu agreed, and extensive discussions were later conducted, with Italian officials mediating the Ethiopia-Tigre dispute and The Carter Center negotiating between the Eritreans and Mengistu's officials.

Later I was asked by Israeli officials to intercede with Mengistu to secure emigration permits for about 3,500 Ethiopian Jews, known as Falasha, or "exiles," who were being prohibited from leaving Ethiopia to go to Israel. I learned what I could about them before approaching the Ethiopian leader. This was the remainder of a group of about 15,000, the others having been transported to Israel some years earlier. The Falasha claim to be descendants of Menelik I, son of the biblical King Solomon and the queen of Sheba, and many of their worship practices have remained unchanged since the times of the prophets. Their Scriptures are not in Hebrew but in another ancient Semitic tongue, and the Falasha still offer animal sacrifices. When I broached the subject of the Falasha's emigration with Mengistu, he agreed to release them provided the government of Israel made a direct request. Eventually this was done, and the Falasha were united in the Holy Land.

I knew that Mengistu was well educated and had received some of his training in the United States, but he always insisted on speaking Amharic, conversing with me through an interpreter. Later an American told me about an interesting event that occurred when he was visiting Mengistu. When a waiter came into the office to take orders for refreshments, the interpreter and the president both requested "chi," while the Westerner, desiring the same drink, said "tea." The visitor wondered aloud about the difference, and Mengistu said casually in English, "Well, there must be an etymological explanation."

When the Tigrean guerrillas took Addis Ababa in 1991, Mengistu fled to Zimbabwe, where he still lives in exile despite unsuccessful attempts by his successors to extradite him to be tried for murder.

I have been willing to deal with Mengistu and others considered international pariahs, since government officials would not communicate directly with them and they are often the only ones who can resolve a serious problem. In most cases, they are eager to have some contact with the Western world, and their status as international outcasts makes them quite reluctant to alienate me by lying.

Certainly some of the people with whom I've dealt have been dictators, killers, and violators of human rights. No one could defend the moral codes of such people, or claim that ethical distinctions among governments cannot or should not be drawn. I realize that the primary "code" of some political leaders is simply to continue enjoying the benefits of power.

The question is, what do we do about it? Do we refuse to talk to such oppressors and simply impose sanctions or trade embargoes on their nations in an effort to apply pressure on them? If so, we deprive the children in those countries of food and medicine, causing needless suffering of innocents. The dictator himself doesn't suffer, and his children and grandchildren get all the food and medicine they need. One unwanted result of such trade embargoes is that we sometimes make a hero of the dictator who is defying the American giant, while he blames his nation's ills on the embargo itself. This has been the result of our unfortunate and counter-productive policy toward Cuba.

The alternative is to focus on pragmatic goals: to prevent war, to reduce suffering, and to open up and bring positive change to cruel or repressive regimes. Often this can be done only if we are willing to communicate with the people in power, however unsavory they may be. Only our willingness to have a dialogue enables us to find room for compromises that can save lives and even, in some cases, induce the dictators to mend their ways.

Sometimes I find that leaders we brand as "evil" are willing to work seriously with us for the sake of peace. North Korean President Kim Il Sung was such a person. When I was serving on a submarine in the Pacific Ocean

during the Korean War, I blamed him as the one who had
caused the conflict. I approached our meeting in 1994 with
trepidation and some degree of animosity, but I found him
to be a man who wanted to end the nuclear crisis and begin
a fruitful series of discussions with the United States.

Much the same situation existed with Gen. Raoul Cedras in Haiti. He was seeking a way out of a political and
military quagmire. But because he and his political associates had been branded as totally evil and excluded from
direct communication with the U.S. government, he had
no way to redeem himself or to correct an evil situation.

I can't claim that I changed the hearts of Kim or Cedras,
or that I "redeemed" them in any spiritual sense. That is
not the point of our peacemaking efforts. The point is to
change their approach to a problem, their behavior.

Although forgiveness is taught in the Bible, I don't draw
a parallel between this religious principle and these activities of The Carter Center. We are not in the business of
forgiving anyone. We only attempt to resolve crises and
prevent the repetition or continuation of illicit acts.

I am sometimes asked, "How can you trust the word of
these men?" The unusual position I hold gives me significant leverage over the leaders of certain pariah states.
Today, for example, President Mobutu Sese Seko in Zaire
is something of an outcast, forbidden to enter the United
States or most of the European nations. Yet his cooperation
is vital in resolving problems of war and refugee flight
in neighboring Rwanda and Burundi. Since I am one of
the few Westerners who is willing to meet with Mobutu, he
now views me—as Mengistu and Cedras did—as one of the

few means through which potentially beneficial negotiations can be conducted. If we at The Carter Center were to announce that Mobutu is unwilling to negotiate seriously or to move toward democracy in Zaire, it would be a serious blow to his remaining credibility on the world scene. Many times I assume that a person is untrustworthy, since he is known to have broken promises in the past. In these cases, I attempt to understand what is in his best interest, analyze our own goals, and then try to connect the two. If I can convince the leader that what we want to achieve is also best for him, then we have a good chance for agreement. In my experience few leaders have broken the promises they have finally made.

One of the most intense negotiations in which I have been involved occurred when, with approval from the White House, I went to Haiti on Saturday, September 17, 1994, with Sen. Sam Nunn and Gen. Colin Powell to try to prevent an armed invasion of the island by 30,000 U.S. troops who were poised for action. Haitian military leaders, headed by Gen. Cedras, had overthrown the elected president, Jean-Bertrand Aristide, who was living in exile in the United States. An old and distinguished man, Emile Jonassaint, was serving temporarily as president.

It was the policy of the United States to communicate only with Haitian leaders whom we recognized, and this meant that, officially, Aristide and his cabinet (all in exile) were the sole official government. The U.S. ambassador in

Port-au-Prince was prohibited from exchanging a written note or even indirect messages with Jonassaint and members of his cabinet. But we were free to discuss the issues with anyone in Haiti.

The key issue was whether the acting president, his cabinet, Cedras and his top staff, and the head of the state police would all resign from office and allow the return to power of the elected president. A previously negotiated agreement plus two UN Security Council resolutions spelled out the precise terms, and all had to be honored. We negotiated for hours with General Cedras and the other military and political leaders, but there were always remaining obstacles to a final agreement. We reached deadlock on several key issues. Cedras was willing to resign voluntarily the following year, but not immediately or under pressure. The top military officials also demanded that Aristide officially issue a bill of amnesty. None was willing to leave the country, maintaining that sending any citizen into exile was a violation of the Haitian constitution. At about 3:00 Sunday morning, we decided to adjourn our session, to get some rest and reconsider our proposals.

I find it helpful to establish some kind of personal relationship with key adversaries, so I made a point of engaging Cedras in a more relaxed conversation. As our small group was leaving the room, he told me that he had not been home for several days, and that he had missed the tenth birthday of his youngest son. I sympathized with his inability to act as a proper father, and we recalled that Rosalynn and I had met him and some of his children four years earlier, when we served as monitors of the election in which Aristide became president. At that time, Colonel Cedras was in charge of security for the election.

Although we were never informed of exactly when the military attack would be launched, everyone knew that an American invasion was imminent. I thought it would not come before Monday evening. Quite early Sunday morning I called Rosalynn just to tell her that I was OK but that we were not making any progress in the negotiations. She said, "Jimmy, you need to talk with General Cedras's wife, because she has a great influence on him." So we made arrangements to visit their home, and our negotiating team arrived there at eight o'clock.

We were introduced to the Cedras's seventeen-year-old son, I autographed a photograph of me and their thirteen-year-old daughter taken during the 1990 election, and I gave a pocketknife as a birthday present to their youngest son. Then the general's wife dismissed the children. It was immediately obvious to us that the petite Yannick Cedras was a powerful force in their family.

While we and her husband remained silent, Mrs. Cedras told us that she had been up all night getting ready for our visit. She complained fervently that Americans didn't acknowledge the grandeur of Haiti. She pointed out that Haiti was the oldest black republic on earth; that it had become independent in 1804 when a small group of slaves under inspired leadership defeated the French army, the finest in the world, and drove the French from Haiti. She deplored the poverty of her country and the divisions that had created strife among the people. She said that her father and grandfather had been offered the presidency of Haiti but had refused to go into politics; they wanted to serve the people in other ways. She also said that the Haitians have great pride, and there was no way that foreign invaders could come into their country without any self-respecting Haitian offering his or her life in defense.

She had seen an American special forces team surreptitiously surveying their house and believed that it would be one of the first targets when the invasion came. Mrs. Cedras told us that the previous night she had brought her three children to the room where we were sitting, and they had taken an oath that they would not leave their home but would stay there and die. Finally she said, "There is no way that we will yield." Her presence was overwhelming, and when she finished speaking, all of us remained silent for a minute or two.

Obviously, we thought our mission had failed. I thanked Mrs. Cedras for her frankness and her forceful presentation, and then nodded to General Powell. As the former chairman of the U.S. Joint Chiefs of Staff, he was highly respected by the Haitian military leaders. He said that there were two choices a commander could make when facing overwhelming forces. Either he could commit suicide, in effect, by sacrificing his life and the lives of all those who trusted him, or he could exercise judgment and wisdom by yielding to the superior forces and preserving his life and his troops for another day.

Then I pointed out the difference between waging

peace and waging war. Peace is much more difficult, I said, because it is more uncertain, continuing, and complex. It is easier to say, once and for all, "I know that the forces we face are overwhelmingly superior, but I will give my life for my country, and I'll also permit my family and many of those who look to me for leadership to die with me." I assured General Cedras that he and his military associates would be treated with respect, as we had promised in the written document over which we had been negotiating.

There was a long and very uncomfortable silence, but Mrs. Cedras finally looked at her husband and nodded silently. Then he said, "OK, we'll meet you in our headquarters in about an hour." This was just one step toward success, but it was a crucial one. I'll never understand completely, but I believe the key factors in the Haitians' decision to resume talks were the inexorability of a massive invasion, their desire to prevent bloodshed, and our pledge that the top military officers would be treated fairly and permitted to work with the leaders of the invading force until the time specified for President Aristide's return to Haiti.

However, back with the military leaders, we were still unable to reach agreement after several hours. Then, Cedras's key assistant burst into the room and announced that U.S. paratroopers were boarding planes to attack Haiti. This news was astonishing to us. The Haitian generals accused us of having misled them by preventing their preparations for an invasion while we professed to be talking peace. Cedras and his associates said that they were breaking off the discussions and leaving to marshal their troops. As a last, desperate ploy, I suggested that we lay the issues before Acting President Jonassaint, so that the civilian leaders could make the final decision.

They reluctantly agreed, and we quickly left through a back door of the large building and entered several armored cars. We drove around an enormous square, filled with thousands of angry demonstrators, to the presidential palace.

Emile Jonassaint was universally ridiculed in America as an aged puppet of Haiti's military dictators. But Rosalynn and I had met him when we had been in Haiti to help monitor two elections, and we knew him as the longtime chief justice of the Haitian Supreme Court and the author of the nation's first democratic constitution. He obviously had the respect of both the civilian and military leaders of the "provisional" government. I explained to Jonassaint and his key cabinet leaders the issues on which we had not been able to agree, while General Cedras and his military associates listened attentively. Knowing that the invasion had already been launched, Jonassaint said simply, "The decision has been made. Haiti chooses peace, not war." Some of his cabinet officers objected strongly and threatened to resign, but he was firm in his commitment. It was his personal courage that prevented a massive military confrontation in Haiti.

By telephone, President Clinton and other top U.S. officials approved our faxed agreement and cleared it with President Aristide, who was in Washington. Finally, after sixty-one planes loaded with paratroopers had been on the way to attack for more than an hour, Emile Jonassaint and I signed the agreement. President Clinton then aborted the operation and ordered the U.S. planes and paratroopers to return to their base.

The next morning, after our team had returned to Washington, a massive military force entered Haiti peacefully, with General Cedras assisting the U.S. commanders to preserve order in the country. Subsequently, I helped to arrange for the Cedras family to move to Panama before President Aristide was scheduled to return. We also ensured that proper compensation was made for the property that the Cedras family agreed to abandon.

The crisis was resolved, and the elected leaders returned to Haiti the following month to assume office.

Earlier in 1994, a serious problem had developed halfway around the world when North Korea persisted in plans to process high-grade uranium, which could be used for warheads in nuclear weapons. When inspectors of the International Atomic Energy Agency were expelled from the country, the global community became deeply concerned, and the United States initiated an effort in the UN Security Council to impose sanctions against North Korea.

For three years, North Korea's President Kim Il Sung had been asking me to come to Pyongyang so that he could explain his position. Now I was informed by Chinese and other experts that North Korea was likely to go to war if the sanctions resolution was approved. They could not accept the branding of their country as an outlaw nation and of their revered, almost worshiped, president as a criminal. The U.S. State Department had been unwilling to approve my intercession, but President Clinton finally gave me permission to make the effort.

Rosalynn and I went first to Seoul to reassure the South Korean leaders about our intentions; then we crossed the demilitarized zone, went to Pyongyang to meet with Kim and other leaders, and returned to South Korea. We were the first people in forty-three years to make this round trip.

During our hours of private conversation in Pyongyang, it was obvious that President Kim was willing to find a way to resolve the differences that had caused the crisis. We knew him as a communist dictator who had precipitated the Korean War and kept his people almost completely isolated from the outside world for more than forty years. But now we heard him extol the virtues of the Christian missionaries who had saved his life when he was a prisoner of the Japanese, promise to cease processing nuclear fuel, express a strong desire for good relations with the United States, and offer to return the remains of all Americans buried in his country during the Korean War.

Although at the time I had no way to confirm his sincerity, I knew that all these commitments would soon be put to the test through Kim's own actions and official U.S.–North Korea negotiations. In addition to being transmitted to Washington, the agreements were announced to the world in a CNN International telecast. It seemed that our mission was completely successful. Not only did the North Koreans agree to cease processing nuclear fuel and to permit the international inspectors to return, but the North Korean president also authorized me to invite South Korean President Kim Young Sam to an unprecedented summit meeting.

Unfortunately, within a month, Kim Il Sung was dead, and, with uncertainty in North Korea about his successor, some of his personal commitments have not been fulfilled. Despite this setback, steady progress has been made to resolve the nuclear issue and some other urgent problems. However, North Korea is still a closed society, and memories of the Korean War leave bitter resentments among those on the Korean peninsula, in the United States, and elsewhere who suffered grave losses during the conflict.

Sometimes our peace efforts involve situations in which the leaders refuse to deal with government officials. Another problem is that almost all of the major wars now taking place in the world are civil conflicts, not hostilities between sovereign nations. It is often unfeasible for U.S. officials or UN representatives to communicate with a revolutionary group attempting to change or overthrow a regime to which our ambassador is accredited or which is a member of the United Nations. So it falls to representatives of The Carter Center or other nongovernmental organizations to serve as the contact point between the warring parties. Since we maintain our unofficial status, representing only The Carter Center, we are generally acceptable even to the most sensitive or suspicious groups.

Obviously, it is important to be careful not to disturb sensitive political situations, and to avoid any encouragement of human rights abuses or violations of peace. It is a firm policy of The Carter Center not to duplicate or compete with efforts by others, and I obtain personal approval from the president of the United States before initiating a peace effort in which our nation is involved. We always make clear to adversaries that our goal is simply to resolve the issue, and we seek commitments from them to cease all activities that violate human rights or international law.

There are more wars today than ever before. At The Carter Center we monitor them all—usually about 110 conflicts at any given time. Some are fairly dormant, but about seventy erupt into violence each year. Thirty are what we call major wars, in which more than 1,000 deaths have occurred on the battlefield. In modern times, there are almost ten civilian deaths, including many women and children, for each soldier killed. The casualties can be horrendous, as we have observed in Bosnia. Many Americans don't realize that in a number of other countries—including Cambodia, Sudan, Ethiopia, Liberia, Burundi, and Rwanda—they have been much greater.

Experiences like the ones we had in Haiti and Korea illustrate, in successes and in shortcomings, some of the peacemaking principles we have developed over the past decade or so at The Carter Center.

Principles for Peacemakers

1. Strive to have the international community and all sides in any conflict agree to the basic premise that military force should be used only as a last resort.

2. Do not interfere with other ongoing negotiation efforts, but offer intercession as an independent mediator when an unofficial presence is the only viable option.

3. Study the history and causes of the dispute thoroughly. Take advantage of any earlier personal involvement with key leaders and citizens of a troubled nation as a basis for building confidence and trust.

4. Seek help from other mediators, especially those who know the region and are known and respected there. (In Africa, for instance, we join forces with distinguished leaders from that continent.)

5. Be prepared to go back and forth between adversaries who cannot or will not confront each other.

6. Explore all possible beneficial influences on those who have created the problem. Use the news media to bring pressure on recalcitrant parties.

7. Be willing to deal with the key people in any dispute, even if they have been isolated or condemned by other parties or organizations.

8. With sensitive international issues, obtain approval from the White House before sending any Americans to take part in negotiations.

9. Insist that human rights be protected, that international law be honored, and that the parties be prepared to uphold mutual commitments.

10. Be willing to listen to detailed explanations and demands from both sides, even when they seem unreasonable or unrealistic.

11. Ensure that each concession is equaled or exceeded by benefits. Both sides must be able to feel that they have gained a victory.

12. Tell the truth, even when it may not contribute to a quick agreement. Only by total honesty can a mediator earn the trust and confidence of both sides.

13. Be prepared for criticism, no matter what the final result may be.

14. Be willing to risk the embarrassment of failure.

15. Never despair, even when the situation seems hopeless.

We work with many others not only to seek peaceful resolution of conflicts but also to attempt to resolve the root causes of despair by increasing the production of basic food grains, improving health care, and supporting the growth of democracy. At The Carter Center, we don't believe that any peace effort, even if it is successful, will be lasting unless people have some control or influence over their own government. If dictators continue to be in charge, they are very likely to persecute their people and deprive them of equal treatment under the law. Eventually, another war will break out. In many countries, we have helped monitor democratic elections, to assure that they are honest, fair, and safe, and that the results are trusted and accepted by the people.

Often military adversaries vying for political power are so filled with hatred that they cannot bring themselves to seek peace through direct or indirect communication. Even when both sides come to realize that they can't prevail on the battlefield, they still reject our offers to shuttle back and forth between them. In a few cases, free elections provide an alternative. When proposing this, we often rely on self-delusion—a major factor in politics. Almost anyone seeking an elective office is convinced: "If the process is honest and the voters know me and these other jokers who are candidates, *surely* they will vote for *me*."

The Carter Center has developed a reputation for ensuring either that an election will be completely fair or that any fraud will be exposed and condemned. Our initial invitation to serve as monitors often comes from a ruling party that has achieved office through military force and wants us to authenticate its democratic victory, which it usually assumes will be inevitable. Sometimes the initiative comes from adversaries who suspect that the incumbents will try to steal the election. When all the major parties want us to monitor the procedure and we feel that our services are needed, we agree to participate. Although we never seek any legal authority, we gain great influence to correct problems as they develop because both sides soon realize that our public condemnation of their improprieties can be quite damaging and that our judgment on the legitimacy of the election will be accepted as final by the international community.

I consider this service vital in many cases, either to prevent or resolve a conflict or to assure that, with freedom in a new democracy, the will of the people will improve the policies of a formerly authoritarian and abusive government. Only in a democratic country can real, lasting peace take root.

CHAPTER SEVEN

Faith in Action

All of us wonder about our real purpose in life. For a few, this question can become a profound source of anxiety. When we have inner turmoil that needs healing, uncertainty about the meaning of life can grow into an obsession with self-pity or depression. For many people, the best solution is to think of something we can do for someone else.

The Bible says that God will wipe away our tears (Revelation 21:4). Wiping away someone else's tears is sometimes necessary to help us dispel our own. No matter what we seek in life, we are more likely to find it if we are not self-centered but concentrate on something or someone outside ourselves.

In many ways, Rosalynn and I were devastated after my

defeat for reelection as president in 1980. We had really wanted another four years in the White House and had many plans for ourselves and our nation. Now all these hopes were shattered. And, at the age of fifty-six, I was too young to consider retirement.

After a few days of considering other possibilities that didn't appeal to either of us, we decided definitely to return home. We still had no idea what to do, but we learned from our financial trustees that our warehouse business had suffered heavy losses while we were away, and we were almost a million dollars in debt. It seemed that we might have to sell all our farmland to pay what we owed. In about three months, however, a large agricultural corporation decided to enter the peanut market, and they bought our warehouse and six others in the Southeast to give them an adequate supply of this crop. The sale price was almost enough to pay our debts.

When my term in office expired, we moved with Amy back to Plains, where she enrolled in the public school and we became, once again, full and active members of our local church. As we repaired our house and grounds, put a floor in the attic to store possessions accumulated during the past nine years of public service and campaigning, became reacquainted with our farms and woodlands, and settled our urgent business affairs, we also tried to inventory what we might have to invest in a productive future life. We would build The Carter Center and write our memoirs. We also became involved with another interesting and challenging project: Habitat for Humanity.

Working with Habitat for Humanity has changed our

attitude about how we can relate to those who really need help. In building homes with "God's people in need," we follow a few simple rules. Volunteers work side by side with families who have been living in subhuman dwellings. The future homeowners are chosen and most other decisions made by a committee formed within the local community. There is no charity involved, if "free handouts" is the meaning of *charity*. The homeowners must contribute about 500 hours of work on their own and neighbors' houses, and they must also repay the full price of their homes, to which they will then have clear title. This is possible because the houses built by Habitat are relatively inexpensive: much of the construction work is done by volunteers, and Habitat's policy is not to charge interest. This makes monthly payments possible from a very low income, even from a welfare check.

One of the greatest benefits of a decent home is that it gives its owners, often for the first time, a sense of success and fulfillment. Working with other volunteers on tasks ranging from clearing a lot to hanging curtains, laying carpets, sodding a lawn, and planting a garden, the new homeowners come to realize that they can take on difficult tasks and perform them. When they have moved into their own new houses, they are full-fledged citizens, with a new status and additional responsibilities. They must pay taxes, maintain their homes, and seek jobs. Although Habitat cannot guarantee our homeowners employment, some of the volunteers observe their good qualities and often guide them to jobs that can support a new and self-sufficient life.

Habitat for Humanity was founded by Millard and

Linda Fuller. Millard is a dynamic and charismatic lawyer; he and Linda are two of our closest friends. As students at the University of Alabama, Millard and a partner, Morris Dees, set up a number of imaginative entrepreneurial ventures. For example, they collected the best recipes from the mothers of other students and published them in fast-selling books. In addition, they obtained from university records information about every student and sought orders from their parents to deliver cakes or flowers on their children's birthdays. (Morris Dees later became a famous civil rights lawyer and the founder of the Southern Poverty Law Center in Montgomery, Alabama.)

As a young lawyer and entrepreneur, Millard continued to be innovative and enthusiastic, and he was soon a millionaire, with so much money coming in from his business ventures that he gave up his law practice. One day, much to Millard's shock, Linda told him that she was leaving him and going to New York for marriage counseling because he was neglecting his family and seemed interested only in getting rich. Millard followed her and begged her to come back to him. Finally, in desperation, he declared that he would give away all his money and join Linda in any work that they could share.

He kept his promise, and they soon settled on the bi-racial Koinonia Farm. There, for five years, the Fullers joined in building houses for destitute black families. Then they and their four children spent three years in Zaire as missionaries supported by several Christian denominations and continued to develop the idea of organizing Habitat for Humanity.

The Fullers say that Habitat uses the "theology of the hammer" or the "economics of Jesus." By the time this book is published, Habitat will have completed homes for more than 50,000 needy families in about 1,500 communities in the United States and in forty-five foreign countries. Now Rosalynn and I send out a large number of fundraising letters for Habitat, spend occasional days on projects near our home, and join with others for a week each year to build a number of complete homes. To date, we have done this in more than a dozen communities, including New York City; Tijuana, Mexico; the Cheyenne River Sioux reservation in South Dakota; Liberty City in Miami; Philadelphia; Chicago; Winnipeg, Manitoba; Atlanta; Charlotte, North Carolina; and the Watts area in Los Angeles. In 1996, our project site was near Budapest in Hungary, and we plan to be in the Appalachian Mountain region in Kentucky in 1997.

Rosalynn and I enjoy vacations, and we could go to Hawaii or on a Caribbean cruise every summer for about the same amount it costs us to travel to one of the Habitat building sites. But when I look back on the last twelve years or so, I see that some of my most memorable and gratifying experiences were when I joined other volunteers and worked to exhaustion building a house alongside the family who would live there. These exhilarating occasions have been rare in my life, but I have learned that the opportunities are always there, for any of us.

It is difficult to describe the emotions of our Habitat workdays. We see extraordinary commitments and lives changed among formerly forgotten people. On our first project, a nineteen-apartment dwelling in Lower Manhattan, one of our homeowners, a former chef named Roosevelt, was sleeping on the street when we met him. He worked with us on this large and difficult project, and when it was finished he lived on the first floor. Because of his fine character and good work, he became the building superintendent. One day while we were installing the roof, I finished a cold drink and began to crumple the aluminum can. Roosevelt startled me by shouting, "Don't bend the can!" I discovered that this was part of his livelihood; he supported himself and began making his monthly payments by collecting empty cans and bottles.

Later, at one of our projects in Puno, Peru, on the shore of Lake Titicaca, Rosalynn and I observed the local people building their homes far above the tree line, at an altitude of about 13,000 feet. There seemed to be an unspoken assignment of tasks, with the men doing most of the laying of concrete blocks and carpentry work on the homes. The women, some with babies strapped on their backs, were using small chisels and tin cans to dig a channel several hundred yards through solid rock to bring water from a small spring to the new dwellings.

In northwest Nicaragua, we visited a Habitat project with President Daniel Ortega and other Sandinista leaders. There, in an area with an almost pure clay soil too poor for farming, people were living in wide open, three-sided shacks built of limbs and grass. The clay, however, made excellent bricks and roof tiles, and the homeowners and their families were molding thousands of them by hand. A small power saw was used to cut a few boards from the local

trees (which happened to be mahogany), to create roof
trusses held together by twisted strands of used barbed
wire. Only some mortar mix and a few nails had to be pur-
chased, so the cash needed for a house for ten people was
only the equivalent of $300 in U.S. currency. When homes
were completed for every family in the village, the people
continued their new industry: manufacturing and selling
high-quality bricks and roofing tiles to other villages.

I asked a woman who lived in a Habitat home in
Philadelphia what kind of dwelling she had had before. She
replied, "There were just two good things in that old place:
me and my husband." Another woman standing nearby
said, "I've got two teenage sons, whom I rarely saw in the
evenings in my other place. Every time the phone rang, I
thought it was the police calling about my boys. Now,
they're home every night, and they bring their friends to
watch television, play games, or study. They said the other
day that they used to be too ashamed to let anyone know
where they lived."

A Habitat family in Olympia, Washington, had been
living in an abandoned automobile. One of their children
was an eight-year-old boy, who was very excited about getting a new house. When the family was chosen, he jumped
up and down and shouted, "We won! We won! We won!"
After the Habitat home was finished and the family moved
in, the little boy attended a different school. He had always
been in the "slow learners'" class, but when he moved his
records were lost and he was put in a regular class by mistake. No one noticed the error, and at the end of the first
half year, his lowest grade was a B. Now he is still learning

with the smartest students. This is what having a decent home for the first time in life can do.

As I said earlier, Rosalynn's and my primary responsibility is to The Carter Center. One of the bases for this work is to avoid duplicating or competing with what others are doing. This means that if the World Bank, UN agencies, the U.S. government, or Harvard University is dealing effectively with a problem, we turn our attention to other issues. Almost by default, then, much of our overseas work is in Latin America and Africa—regions that tend to be neglected by other governmental and social agencies.

As in Habitat, working on common projects as equals tends to forge almost instantaneous and binding ties among people, regardless of geographic separation or other differences. In the ghetto areas of great cities, on American Indian reservations, and in the villages of Chad, Haiti, Ethiopia, and Sudan, I have seen the emotional effect of sharing an opportunity for a better home, an increased yield of food grains, or relief from a devastating disease. There is an instant and overwhelming melding of cultures, languages, and interests into a spirit of friendship and love.

Much more than when I was president, I now understand the potential benefits from programs among some of the world's poorest people. Unfortunately, relatively little attention is given to these opportunities for our country to demonstrate world leadership by sharing a small portion of our great wealth. For some reason, the words "foreign aid" have become dirty words in politics, to be avoided by any candidate for public office.

There is a dramatic difference between what American citizens believe and want and what our government is doing. A 1995 public opinion poll showed that almost two-thirds of Americans agree that economic growth in poor foreign countries helps us, and that the United States should use part of our wealth to assist less fortunate people abroad. Those surveyed also thought that our foreign aid was, on average, 18 percent of the U.S. budget. The actual figure is less than 1 percent. Norway gives almost 3 percent of its gross national income to humanitarian causes, while the United States gives only one-sixth of 1 percent. Of all the industrialized nations, we are by far the stingiest in sharing our wealth with others. And today the U.S. Congress is making further large reductions in USAID funds for Africa, which are used for food, medicine, the control of AIDS and polio, and the promotion of democracy and peace. This selfish policy betrays the concept of greatness for the world's only superpower.

Despite our government's attitudes, Americans always have been a generous people. Privately, we give more than $4 billion to humanitarian causes in other countries. The work of CARE, Save the Children, and other secular relief organizations is well known. Religious groups, including missionary organizations, play a powerful role as well.

Too often we think about evangelism only as preaching the Gospel, but there is also a powerful ministry in the alleviation of suffering, reaching out in harmony, respect, and partnership to others, and sharing life. One of the most

significant aspects of the ministry of Jesus was the combination of his religious witnessing with his personal service
to those he encountered. His spirit lives on today in the
work of people like Jerome and Joann Ethredge.

In 1976, Jerome Ethredge was an agronomist at the
experiment station near Plains. Always active in the work
of our church congregation, Jerome eventually realized
that he had more to offer than just his service on Sundays
among relatively self-sufficient farmers and neighbors.
With no previous religious experience except as lay members of our church, he and Joann volunteered for full-time
service as Baptist missionaries. After receiving basic religious instruction and French language training, they were
assigned to Togo, in West Africa. The ministry of Jerome
and Joann provides a vivid demonstration of the inseparability of faith and works.

For seven years the Ethredges served in the large town
of Sokodé, where they offered language and other education courses to young people who were willing to visit their
small Christian library. Hundreds learned to read and
write, but few had any interest in the religious aspect of the
center. In time, Jerome and Joann decided they wanted to
move deeper into the agricultural regions, where the needs
were greater and they could use Jerome's experience in
agronomy.

When a new missionary came to Sokodé, the Ethredges
moved to the small village of Moretan, in the East Mono
area of Togo, where most of the people worshiped various
aspects of nature. All attempts by both Muslim and Chris-

tian evangelists in this region had failed. Within sixty miles of their new home, there were only five small Muslim and two Catholic congregations. Jerome and Joann decided to combine Christian witnessing with attempts to alleviate the people's urgent physical needs.

One of the most obvious needs was for drinking water. Some lucky villagers had a water hole even during the dry season, but many lived miles from any supply. In one village, half the women had to walk sixteen miles each day to fetch clay jars of water, alternating this duty with others who cared for all the children and performed the rest of the community chores. With financial support from some Baptists in North Carolina, Jerome began to seek water supplies with a truck-mounted diesel drill. He had to penetrate a regional layer of granite at or near the surface, making the operation slow and tedious. Assisted only by the local residents, he went to every village within eighty miles of his home base and drilled 167 wells, 130 successful and capped with hand pumps. Now every village has a clean and healthy water supply.

During this time, Jerome also used his agronomy skills to increase greatly the production of basic food crops. Recognizing the shortage of protein in the villagers' diets, he acquired a bulldozer and constructed twenty-one deep ponds that fill during the rainy seasons. Located to serve as many villages as possible, the ponds were stocked with fish, and they now provide a continuing new source of food.

While Jerome was busy with these and other projects, Joann worked with families on intensive health and educa-

tion projects. She has helped to build a pharmacy in
Moretan and arranges transportation to a distant regional
hospital for people too ill to be treated locally.

The greatest problem of the East Mono people was that
they were isolated from the rest of Togo during four
months of the rainy season, when the Mono River became
an impassable torrent. Only one small dugout canoe, hewn
from a tree trunk, was available to cross the stream in
emergencies. Working again with local people and his Baptist friends from North Carolina, some of whom came to
Togo as volunteers, Jerome designed and eventually built a
bridge across the river. Rosalynn and I were amazed when
we visited the Ethredges to find a 230-foot concrete span.
It was hard to believe that this vital transportation link had
been built by one missionary and a few volunteers.

All this work has been done in a quiet and self-effacing
way, in complete cooperation with the Togolese people,
and always in the name of Christ. The Ethredges demonstrate their religious faith by their work in classrooms and
health clinics, behind ox-drawn plows, on hospital trips in
a dilapidated van, on a bulldozer, or operating a borehole
drill.

Most of the evangelistic work is now being done by new
Togolese Christians. Each group has a recognized leader
who preaches and organizes Bible teaching and other
church activities. The oldest is just thirty-five years old.
This has been the religious result of the Ethredges' work as
the only Christian missionaries in the region. There are
now eighty-one church congregations in East Mono, with

a total of 5,000 active members, more than one-third of the Baptists in the nation!

Most of The Carter Center's humanitarian programs are in Africa, involved directly with health care and the production of food by small farmers. A few years ago, leaders of the World Health Organization, UNICEF, the World Bank, the UN Development Program, and the Rockefeller Foundation were all striving in their own ways to immunize children throughout the world. However, they were never able to reach more than 20 percent of the total, primarily because they were not cooperating with one another. The Task Force for Child Survival was created and located at The Carter Center so that all five organizations could work as a team. Within only five years, with no appreciable increase in funding or personnel, 80 percent of the world's children were immunized against polio, measles, and other contagious diseases.

The Carter Center has also formed a task force on disease eradication, which is continually analyzing human ailments to ascertain which ones might be totally eradicated. Two—polio and dracunculiasis (guinea worm)—have already been targeted, and others—like measles, yaws, and leprosy—will probably join the list in the near future.

The key to all these efforts is Dr. Bill Foege, a tall, lanky Iowan and devout Lutheran who has combined his deep religious faith with humanitarian work. He is one of the most effective medical doctors on earth in preventing diseases, having been instrumental in the eradication of smallpox in 1977, head of the Centers for Disease Control for almost ten years, and later executive director of The Carter Center. The opportunities for our involvement in health programs come from his inspirational work. He has forgone a high income so that he could continue to serve people in the most remote, seriously afflicted, and often unknown communities in the developing world. Many other health experts are willing to make similar sacrifices just to work with Dr. Foege.

He is a fine companion, with wonderful stories to tell of his experiences in the battle against disease. Once he was in the deep jungle of Biafra during the final stages of smallpox eradication. The challenge was to immunize hundreds of people scattered in small, isolated villages. He went to see the regional chief, explained the program, and asked for a guide to take him to the widespread communities. The chief looked up at the six-foot, seven-inch American and replied, "No, it will be easier if we bring them all here." He directed his drummer to commence sending a message, and the next morning a stream of people crowded into the village square. After they were all immunized, Dr. Foege asked the chief, "How in the world did you induce them to come here just for an immunization program?" The chief replied, "I told them to come if they wanted to see the tallest man in the world."

The opportunity to perform neighborly service for needy people is not limited to individuals, and not all corporate leaders are as hardened toward human illness and death as are the tobacco company executives. It may be a surprise to many readers to learn that American corporations are deeply involved in some of the most effective humanitarian programs in the Third World. I have found that, when corporate leaders understand a problem, they are often quite generous, and their employees are proud and enthusiastic.

Guinea worm is a terrible disease that, until recently, afflicted people in India, Pakistan, Yemen, and nineteen nations across the continent of Africa. Villagers who drink water from stagnant ponds ingest the minuscule eggs that, within a year, grow into worms more than two feet long. These parasites then sting the skin from the inside and emerge, over a period of weeks, through the festering sore. As the sufferer wades into the pond for pain relief or to secure more water, the worms lay thousands of eggs, and the cycle is repeated. There are several ways to eradicate the disease. One is to drill borehole wells that provide pure water, as Jerome Ethredge did in Togo. Another is to put into the water a chemical called Abate, which kills the eggs.

In tests in Pakistan, we learned that using a filter cloth, finely woven and resistant to rot, would be the most effective technique for providing safe, potable water. However, such fibers and fabric did not exist, and even inferior substitutes were very expensive. I went to see Edgar Bronfman, then one of the major owners of DuPont Corporation, and described our problem. He soon brought the issue to DuPont's board of directors, and they agreed to develop a special fiber and provide enough of the cloth,

at no cost to us, for our entire effort. President Lanty
Smith and other executives of Precision Fabrics Company
volunteered to have their production facility weave the
fabric. Later, American Cyanamid Company offered to
give us a worldwide supply of Abate so that we could attack
the problem by treating the water in some smaller ponds.

In 1988, when we began our eradication program, we
found 3.5 million people suffering from guinea worm. As
of the end of 1995, there were only 130,000 cases, with
more than half the total in an area of southern Sudan where
a thirteen-year war has prevented health workers from getting access to many villages.

I went to DuPont headquarters to report on our
progress, where President Ed Woolard and about 600 top
managers, scientists, and salesmen were assembled under a
large tent. When I thanked them for their gift and showed
a brief film demonstrating its almost miraculous results,
most of them were weeping—and so was I.

One of the most profitable medicines marketed by
Merck & Company, the large pharmaceutical firm, is Mectizan, used to prevent heartworm in dogs and other ani-
mals. A few years ago, one of their research scientists
discovered that the same drug was effective for humans.
Just one tablet each year could stop the development of
onchocerciasis, or river blindness. For people living alongside rapidly flowing streams in thirty-six African and Latin
American countries, the sting of a little black fly first causes

a terrible rash like permanent poison ivy. Later there are
splotches on the skin that resemble leprosy, and nodules—
puffed-up places as big as golf balls—develop on the body.
After twelve years, total blindness results.

The chief executive officer of Merck, Dr. Roy Vagelos,
came to The Carter Center and met with Dr. Foege to tell
him about this discovery. He learned that there were more
than 30 million people who needed the treatment. Dr.
Vagelos said that if The Carter Center could develop a procedure to deliver the Mectizan tablets, Merck would provide them to all the affected villages in the world, free of
charge.

To meet this challenge, a very modest but successful
young businessman from Texas, John Moores, established
and personally financed the River Blindness Foundation,
which has helped to distribute a total of 50 million Mectizan
tablets, reaching more than 14$^{1}/_{2}$ million people in 1995.

Rosalynn and I recently accompanied Dr. Vagelos to a
small village in southern Chad where every person had
river blindness; many of them were totally blind. Although
lost sight cannot be restored with the annual tablets, for
those not yet blind the illness will not progress further, and
for everyone in the village, the terrible itching and sores
have disappeared. Onchocerciasis is not a further threat to
them, and they can now move back into the productive
bottomlands near the stream, which they had abandoned to
escape the flies.

These are examples of business executives who, because
of their personal interest, have helped to make possible

the kind of healing that Christ himself exhibited. This corporate generosity has been extremely gratifying, not only for top executives but for all employees. In the main lobby of Merck's headquarters in New Jersey, there is a bigger-than-life statue of a little boy holding one end of a stick, the other end held by his blind father. Everyone who works in this company knows that millions of Africans will never be blind because of their generosity in contributing Mectizan tablets. There are similar opportunities for other leaders in the corporate world.

What was the main thrust of Christ's ministry? Did he just sit under a fig tree telling stories, or stand on a mountain explaining his theology? No. His ministry was tangible proof of his love for everyone, including the sick, the ostracized, and even those who were believed by their neighbors to be suffering the punishment of God for their sins. This was a powerful witness. Christ was a doer, one whose faith took the form of action, not merely words.

It is a real challenge to correlate our religious faith with what we actually do. In his epistle, James says, "For as the body without the spirit is dead, so faith without works is dead also" (James 2:26). James is not suggesting that we should ignore faith and sharing the Good News with others. He is saying that if we have faith, then we must show it by how we live, what we do.

Even in a personal way, we cannot separate faith or belief from our actions or works. When I offered Rosalynn an engagement ring, we both realized that her simple acceptance of it implied the commitment of a lifetime. Similarly, when we accept the free gift of salvation through God's grace, it imposes an obligation—a pleasant one—to serve by striving to live in harmony with his teachings.

Jesus made it plain that he had not come to change "one jot or tittle" of the law (Matthew 5:18), but he went out of his way to demonstrate that a narrow, legalistic interpretation of the Scriptures should not obscure the real meaning of faith in God. He repeatedly forgave and healed people on the Sabbath, reached out to the despised Samaritans and to Roman soldiers and other gentiles, touched lepers and a bleeding woman without considering himself unclean, and condemned merely superficial compliance with the law. These differences with the religious authorities helped lead to his arrest, trial, and crucifixion.

Christ wants us today to follow his example by expanding the meaning of forgiveness, service, and love—all in a practical way. And he goes on to teach that this is the avenue toward personal peace and freedom. We're not putting ourselves in a cage by reaching out to other people—we're doing just the opposite. To me, Christianity is not a submission to restraints; the essence of Christ's teaching is to liberate us and give us peace.

A few blocks from The Carter Center in Atlanta is a place known as Café 458. There, homeless people can get a hug and a warm welcome, sit down at a table, select the meal they prefer, and order it from an attentive waiter. Many of them have serious problems, including addiction

to drugs or alcohol. The eleven volunteers, who live next
door, get to know the "guests" well enough to refer them
to treatment centers or to work with them directly.

A salesman, A. B. Short, and his wife, Ann Conner, a
nurse-practitioner, opened the café in 1988, knowing that
many people needed help but also realizing that standing in
soup lines every day offered little permanent benefit.

The guests make table reservations for a month at a
time, with extensions provided they are working steadily
toward the goals they have set for improving their lives.
More than 1,600 people have passed through Café 458, in
the process regaining some of their dignity as human
beings, and many of them now help as volunteers. Among
those who have been through the drug rehabilitation program, only 8 percent have relapsed.

One man named Roy said he had slept in a Dunkin'
Donuts Dumpster for ten years before being welcomed at
Café 458. He then stopped selling cocaine, took a job with
a landscaping company, made foreman in six months, and
began to believe in God. He finally met his daughter, and
he no longer lives in an enormous trash container. Treated
with care and respect, Roy has found a new life.

Many of the people mentioned in this book are fairly
well known, but publicity is not necessary for an inspirational life. We recognize Mother Teresa, Billy Graham,
Pope John Paul II, and others who have become famous
because, in their own ways, they have demonstrated their
Christian faith. But Rosalynn and I have had many friends,

most of them unknown except among their close neighbors, who have been able to live their faith by combining
the apparently conflicting elements of strength and gentleness. These are the people who have motivated us and
helped to transform our lives.

When I was growing up in Archery, a fine young woman
named Annie Mae Hollis worked for my parents. After I
left home for college, she moved to Albany, Georgia, where
she married a man named Rhodes and got a job helping in
a wealthy woman's house.

When my father was terminally ill, Mother called Annie
Mae and said, "I can't nurse Earl and take care of all the
family at the same time. Could you come back and help
me?" So Annie Mae moved back to Plains to be with our
family. I will never forget that when my father breathed his
last breath on July 22, 1953, Annie Mae Rhodes was
holding him in her arms.

Annie Mae had a good life. Because of her sterling
qualities, she never lacked a job, and she became almost a
full member in the families she served as a maid. She was a
stalwart member of her church and a counselor to others in
her congregation. She owned her small but attractive
home, which was a focal point for socializing, especially
among her family. Her handicapped brother lived with her,
able to move around, mostly in his wheelchair, and even
assist in the household chores.

In July 1994, Annie Mae was sleeping when, in the
middle of the night, her brother woke her and said, "It's
been raining for hours, and the radio says the water's
coming." She said, "The water's not coming. I've been here

thirty-seven years, and water's never come in my house."
But he insisted, so she got up, found her Bible, and tried to
pull her old dog out of the house. Before she could get to
the car, the water was waist deep, so she clung to the car
door handle until some rescue workers picked her and her
brother up in a boat. Her dog drowned, and her car, her
house, and everything in it were destroyed. Annie Mae lost
all she had, except a Bible and the small and now water-
ravaged lot where her house had stood.

Rosalynn and I were in Japan when we heard about the
flood, and we didn't know anything about Annie Mae's
plight. Two women from Atlanta went down to Albany
within a couple of days to help in the relief work, and they
met this extraordinary seventy-seven-year-old woman,
who was hobbling around trying to see what was left of her
community. She was helping to rejuvenate everybody's
spirits by saying, "We need not be concerned. The Lord
will take care of us. We have to have faith in God and in
ourselves."

The two women were so impressed with Annie Mae
Rhodes' faith that they asked about her life. She mentioned
in passing that she had worked for our family about forty
years ago, but she said, "Don't bother Mr. Jimmy. I don't
want to be a burden to him." Nonetheless, the women
wrote me a letter and described what had happened.

Some of us volunteers with Habitat for Humanity
helped Annie Mae build a small new house on her lot, for
which she will have a clear title by making monthly payments. She has decided, since she's elderly and doesn't have
any children, and since her brother is also quite old, that

she's going to deed the house back to Habitat when she passes away.

Annie Mae's simple faith, expressed in works, is what James describes in his New Testament epistle: "My brothers and sisters, whenever you face trials of any kind, consider it nothing but joy, because you know that the testing of your faith produces endurance; and let endurance have its full effect, so that you may be mature and complete, lacking in nothing" (James 1:2–4). Most of us don't know from personal experience how people like Annie Mae Rhodes live in potential flood plains, the ghettos of America's cities, or the Third World nations of Sierra Leone, Ethiopia, Haiti, Niger, or Chad. But James tells us to let our religious faith inspire us to help alleviate their suffering.

People like the Ethredges, Bill Foege, Roy Vagelos, A. B. Short, Ann Conner, and Annie Mae Rhodes show that simple acts can be transforming and highly significant. Life is made up of an accumulation of habits, shaped by the day-by-day, hour-by-hour decisions that we make. There's a need for me, as a Christian, to take a look at myself and my relationship to others, and ask whenever I make a decision, "What would Christ do?" When I remember and act accordingly, my life can be made more resistant to worry, fear, frustration—and boredom!

"Enduring faith" describes Annie Mae Rhodes, who survived the flood that destroyed her home. But what would I do under the stress of a terrible loss? Could I be equally resilient, forceful, courageous, and innovative, not based on my own physical strength or intelligence or ability to borrow money or to buy another house, but based upon my faith in God? What was Annie Mae's most important possession—an automobile that has now been hauled off and crushed, an old dog, a modest house that is now just a pile of splintered lumber, or her religious faith, which sustained her in a crisis? Hundreds of flood victims and rescue workers were inspired by the quiet faith of a stooped, confident, quiet seventy-seven-year-old woman.

CHAPTER EIGHT

Crossing Barriers

It is perfectly legitimate and even admirable for Americans to promote their personal values through either religious or political processes. As I have said elsewhere in this book, the role of spiritual leaders in America's civil rights movement is a wonderful example of the healing role faith can play in our national life. But when we attempt to use our government to force others to worship as we do, or treat those who differ as second-class citizens, then we are violating the basic tenets of a democracy.

Unfortunately, many people of faith today focus more on the quarrels that divide us than on the values that unite us. As a traditional Baptist, I am deeply concerned about arguments that have driven wedges between members of our denomination. I know and respect many devout believers who accept every word in the Bible as literally true. In a number of American school systems, in state legislatures, and in the federal courts, the debate rages about whether creationism should be taught in high school science classes. Even though some people are obsessed with both sides of these issues, arguing them is fruitless.

Christians can buttress their arguments on almost any subject by emphasizing certain selected Scripture verses and then claiming that they should be applied universally. But when we do this, we're using the Bible as a rationalization for our personal preferences, which we assume are correct. The resulting divisions are usually based on the presumption of preeminence by one group over others: "God and I are right, and anyone who disagrees with us is wrong." I'm always concerned about such "true believers."

About twenty years ago, some of these Christians began to forge a political union with the more conservative wing of the Republican party. This wedding between the political and the religious would have conflicted with my belief in separation of church and state even if it had been with Democrats.

Now leaders of the highly organized Christian Right have successfully injected into America's political debate some divisive questions. The most vivid examples involve sexual preference, which obviously has highly personal and emotional overtones. The focus seems to be colored by political considerations. For example, almost all Protestants, including many allied with the Christian Right, will now acknowledge divorce as an acceptable choice for unhappy couples, and they rarely speak out against "fornication" or adultery, although Jesus repeatedly condemned these acts. It is much easier and more convenient for heterosexual Christians to attack homosexuals, based primarily on selected verses in the Old Testament. They fail to acknowledge that homosexuality was never mentioned by Jesus.

Some prominent Christian leaders even claim that AIDS is God's special punishment on sinners and that AIDS victims should be treated accordingly. In the time of Jesus, many thought this way about people with leprosy, who were also looked upon as condemned by God and capable of contaminating their neighbors. Jesus set an example for us by reaching out to them, loving and healing them.

Other Christians and the general public must not condone, even by silence, the judgmental attitudes promoted by a few demagogic religious and political leaders. That a premise originates within the religious community tends to authenticate it among those who want to justify their personal prejudices. It would be a tragedy if a platform of "I hate gay men and women" proved to be a route to political office in the United States of America.

The Gospels make it clear that dividing and despising people according to sexual behavior, religious or ethnic background, or other personal traits was never Jesus' way. The fourth chapter of John's Gospel describes a significant encounter between Jesus and a Samaritan woman. She was known as promiscuous, having lived with five "husbands" in succession, and was condemned by her own people. She never went to the well during the cooler hours of the day with the other women but went at noon, by herself. We can imagine that the other women walked together, exchanged the gossip of the village, and talked about their children or grandchildren while she watched from her window until they came back to their homes.

Furthermore, this woman was a Samaritan. The Samaritans were Jews whose ancestors were Abraham, Isaac, and Jacob and who worshiped the same Almighty God as all other Jews. However, the Samaritans were convinced that only five books belonged in the Bible, and they recognized Moses as the only prophet. They looked upon Mt. Gerizim, not Jerusalem, as their holy place. When the Israelites returned home from exile, some of those who had stayed in Samaria had intermarried with gentiles, and these were excluded from rebuilding Jerusalem.

Subsequently, the Samaritans were despised outcasts who were considered to have betrayed their religion. An Israelite on whom a Samaritan's shadow had fallen required ceremonial cleansing before he or she could enter the temple to worship.

One day, while his disciples were away buying food, Jesus approached the Samaritan woman and said, "Will you give me a drink?" Although its significance may not be obvious at first, this simple act was a startling demonstration against racial or religious prejudice. All Southerners who lived during the time of racial segregation can recognize its bold nature. As a child, when my parents were away on a trip, I lived, ate, and slept with our African-American neighbors, Jack and Rachel Clark. My black boyhood friends and I played and went fishing together, plowed with mules side by side, and played on the same baseball team.

But when I carried water to a group of people working in the field, it would have been inconceivable for black workers and white ones, including me, to drink out of the same dipper. For Jesus to drink from the Samaritan woman's cup was a powerful symbolic act of acceptance and friendship.

Amazed by Jesus' openness to her, the Samaritan woman engaged him in conversation, and, after just a few minutes of simple talk, she became convinced that Jesus was the Messiah.

During her brief encounter with Jesus, a miracle occurred—not a physical miracle but a spiritual one. Because Jesus broke down all the racial, social, and religious barriers between them, this woman became a messenger around whom the villagers gathered to hear the Good News about a man whom they soon knew as "truly the Savior of the world." The encounter between Christ and the Samaritan woman is one of the most gratifying examples of salvation in the Bible. This woman was given what she needed most: acceptance, forgiveness, and a new life.

Unfortunately, we are usually quite comfortable with our prejudices. In my book *Turning Point* I described the racial discrimination that existed over thirty years ago in the Deep South. At that time segregation was legally enforced. But although the laws have changed, our society now is almost as segregated as it was then, not just in the South but in Boston, Chicago, Los Angeles, and New York City.

Christians and believers of every faith have a responsibility to help break down barriers based on race, sex, religion, and other differences. Jesus used just one cup of water to demonstrate the overcoming of prejudice. We have opportunities to do the same.

When Paul wrote, "There is no longer Jew or Greek, there is no longer slave or free, there is no longer male and female; for all of you are one in Christ Jesus" (Galatians 3:28), he was expressing a revolutionary tenet of Christianity. This was a leveling of the ground, an uplifting of those who felt despised, and a warning to those who considered themselves superior. Notice that Paul included gender as one of the distinctions no longer to be recognized by believers. Most people don't claim publicly the right to discriminate against those who are poor, those who come from Asia or South America, or those whose skin is black or brown. But many still maintain the right to discriminate against people because they are female.

There was gross discrimination against women in ancient times. They were often treated as chattel, or worse. Demosthenes, a famous Greek orator and writer, described the attitude of the men who belonged to one of the competitive religious cults that worshiped a goddess: "Our mistresses are for pleasure. Our concubines are to meet our day-to-day bodily needs. Our wives are to produce legitimate children and to be trusted guardians of our homes."

By contrast, Jesus ministered to women, even to prostitutes, and exalted them in general to be equal with men in his service. We know from the New Testament that it was the women who helped care for Jesus during his ministry.

Unlike the male disciples, who fled in fear of their lives, the women were there when he was crucified: "There were also women looking on afar off: among whom was Mary Magdalene, and Mary the mother of James, and Salome; who also, when he was in Galilee followed him, and ministered unto him, and many other women which came up with him unto Jerusalem" (Mark 15:40, 41). Not only that, but we know from Paul and Peter, as they wrote their epistles, that after Christ's death, women played the roles of preachers, missionaries, disciples, and leaders in the Church.

Many early translators of the biblical texts chose words that prescribed a lesser role for women, expressing the male-dominant attitudes that prevailed in their societies at the time. The same prejudice continues today, with some contemporary religious leaders even extrapolating from the temptation of Eve in Genesis to a condemnation of all women as responsible for original sin.

In some states today, the official Baptist policy is to expel from the convention any church that ordains a woman as pastor and to condemn those that have women serving as deacons. In one of our major seminaries, in fact, where I had made the graduation speech the previous year, the new fundamentalist president began firing all professors who believed that women should be permitted to serve as deacons or ministers.

Those who believe in repressing the aspirations of women like to find Bible verses that seem to support their position. It is true that, under certain local circumstances, the apostle Paul made statements that seem to restrict the activities of Christian women. Perhaps these ideas were derived from his background as a Pharisee or were designed to resolve specific social problems in a troubled New Testament church. In a letter to the Ephesians, Paul wrote, "Wives, submit yourselves unto your husbands, as unto the Lord. For the husband is the head of the wife, even as Christ is head of the church." But he added, "Husbands, love your wives, even as Christ also loved the church, and gave himself for it. . . . So ought men to love their wives as their own bodies. He that loves his wife loves himself. . . . Let every one of you in particular so love his wife even as himself; and the wife see that she reverence her husband" (Ephesians 5:23–33).

This prescription of *equal* love between husband and wife was a startling improvement over the way wives had been treated in ancient times. But for too long, and among all too many Christians, these and a few other verses have been selectively quoted by men to prevent equal opportunities for women to serve our Savior. Paul's admonition to women to "submit" is an anomaly among the attitudes of Jesus and other New Testament texts, including other more definitive writings of Paul.

In the sixteenth chapter of his epistle to the Romans, Paul mentions the people who played a significant role in the early church's ministry. Ten of the twenty-seven listed are women, and they were top leaders by any standard. He referred to Phoebe as a minister or deacon (not a "deaconess"), Junia as "outstanding among the apostles," and Priscilla and her husband as co-pastors of a church that worked with Paul, "laid down their own necks" for his life, and corrected the Christian beliefs of Apollos, himself a great preacher.

There are similar instances throughout the New Testament, demonstrating vividly that Jesus brought a revolutionary status of equality to women. One of the most remarkable examples is Mary Magdalene, who was cured of her afflictions by Jesus. She became one of the most valued helpers during his ministry, traveling with the disciples and raising money to pay expenses, and, as I noted before, she was extraordinarily loyal and courageous, even when the men abandoned Jesus. We know that Mary Magdalene was present when Jesus was crucified and accompanied his body to the tomb. Most dramatically, she was the first Christian witness after the resurrection of Jesus, who went and announced to the others, "I have seen the Lord."

Most Baptist men have long recognized the inspired leadership of women in our church congregations, in serving other members in countless ways, and in supporting missionary programs, fulfilling the highest commands of our Savior. In almost every case, the dedication and effectiveness of women as Christians have exceeded the contributions of men.

But this has had little effect on the fundamentalists who have taken control of the Southern Baptist Convention. In 1984, they pushed through a resolution denying the ordination of women because "man was first in creation and woman was first in the Edenic [Garden of Eden] fall." This ridiculous statement, based on a convoluted interpretation of some verses in the Book of Genesis, is now the official policy of Southern Baptists.

Although each church congregation is still considered to be autonomous, this decision has had a far-reaching effect. There are approximately 3,350 Baptist churches in Georgia, of which only one has a female pastor. A graduate of the Candler School of Theology at Emory University, she has been serving a small congregation just ten miles from Plains for about a year. During her brief ministry, eight new members have been added to her church, a 35 percent increase. Unfortunately, her church is not a member of our forty-five-church Friendship Association, having been denied membership seven years ago when they elected some women to serve as deacons.

Recently I told an audience about a neighbor of ours, a Methodist pastor assigned to a little church called Morningside. When Rev. Jackson-Adams came, there were only eighteen church members, with just one child in the whole congregation. The new pastor asked the district superintendent, "Why have you given me a church that's heavily in debt and only has a few older members, none of whom are financially able to meet our budget?" The district superintendent replied, "Well, you can't go wrong. Anything you can figure out to close down that church by next December, we will accept. And we will be proud of you because you did it harmoniously."

Rev. Jackson-Adams prayed about it and remembered that in the seminary graduating class there were some Korean students who were ordained as ministers. In Korea, each graduate of a seminary must go to a community and form a new congregation. So the pastor thought about it and decided, "Why don't we try, in effect, to start a church?" The members began visiting families in the community, and by December the church was out of debt. The sanctuary was now almost full. Within another year, Morningside had over 215 members, with even more attending the worship services. They soon had to have two morning services every Sunday and began planning a larger building.

Some local Baptists are discomfited because Rev. Jackson-Adams's first name is Virginia. But this pastor—Jenny, to us—has proven the great, and special, contribution that women have to make in a Christian church, even in a very conservative community like ours.

Although I am a member of Maranatha Baptist Church, which is affiliated with the Southern Baptist Convention, I don't feel exclusively loyal to a particular Christian denomination. In fact, looking back on my life, I remember most favorably the close interrelation among the churches in our hometown. My mother was a Methodist and my father a Baptist; Rosalynn was a Methodist, her mother a Baptist who joined the Methodists to be with her husband; Rosalynn's grandfather was a Baptist and his wife a Lutheran.

Until the mid-1950s, the Plains churches were part-time and our families alternated our church attendance: the first and third Sundays of the month, we went to the Baptist church; the second and fourth Sundays to the Methodist church; and some people, including Rosalynn's family, went to the Lutheran church on fifth Sundays.

Now, among those who attend my Sunday school class at Maranatha, only about 15 percent are Baptists. In addition, many Jews and other non-Christians join us in our Habitat work.

I feel especially sympathetic with the basic religious beliefs of the Mennonites and the Amish, two groups I know well. To me, the essential beliefs of all Christians, including Protestants, Catholics, and Orthodox Christians, are fundamentally compatible. Although a matter of controversy and concern to some, denominational divisions or distinctions are not important in my daily life and actions.

As we learn in the Book of Acts, the few and embattled believers in the early Christian church were united by their euphoric and inspirational sense of the presence of the Holy Spirit. Jesus had lived just a few years earlier and was still described in vivid terms by people who had actually known him. His disciples had walked the dusty streets of the Holy Land with him, had slept in fields with him, had been tired and persecuted with him, had abandoned him during the last few hours of his life, and had then been reunited and inspired by his resurrection. All this shared life experience was a powerful influence for harmony among the early Christians.

But as the church grew in numbers and influence, sharp divisions arose. People considered their own talents or spiritual gifts to be superior. There were ethnically based arguments between Jews and gentiles who had become followers of Christ, and the Christians squabbled over how to share wealth between the rich and poor. They argued about which of the apostles was most prestigious—Paul,

Peter, or Apollos. Some claimed that it was necessary first to be circumcised before becoming a Christian, others that it was not. Was it permissible to eat meat that had been offered to idols, even though the idols were only pieces of carved wood or metal? Questions like these divided the early church. These Christians had let the overarching concepts of faith, love, and forgiveness be obscured by arguments about exactly what was written or said or remembered about past history.

Unfortunately, after 2,000 years of studying and debating these kinds of issues, the Christian church now is probably divided worse than it was in those early days. In almost all denominations, various beliefs have torn us apart, and sometimes entire denominations have split permanently and officially. As a result, there are lawsuits in many states about who has control of a church building or which group has the authority to choose a pastor. There are "inerrantists," who think that every word in the Bible, preferably the King James Version, is literally true. To argue about matters of this kind is divisive and counterproductive, but they are still burning issues within the fundamentalist Christian community.

Looking at the experiences of today, I can imagine a hypothetical church in New Testament times, where 52 percent might have said Peter meant "so-and-so," 30 percent said the opposite, and 18 percent had no opinion. So the 52 percent took over, and then what happened? The 30 percent split off and formed their own congregation. That may have been the first Baptist church!

To outside observers, the divisions among Christians

are incomprehensible and scandalous. While we preach love for one another as a foundation of our faith, many of the leaders of our religious factions vituperate other groups of believers. There is no doubt that most Christians are also dismayed by these disputes.

Recently, I asked my Sunday school class members to list the items that now seem to be supported or condemned most enthusiastically within our various Christian denominations, and they quickly named abortion, homosexuality, mandatory prayer in public schools, use of public funds to support religious education, the ordination of women as priests or church officials, the inerrancy of the Bible, the priesthood of believers, the autonomy of local congregations, the glorification of pastors, and the breakdown of barriers between church and state. All these issues are important and worth debating, but none should become the basis of hatred and exclusion among believers.

I also disagree with Christians who promote the doctrine that God decides in advance who will be accepted—who will be the chosen or "the elect." There is an element of arrogance in making the claim "I have been chosen by God, others have not." The New Testament clearly states, "It is not the Lord's will for any to be lost, but for all to come to repentance" (2 Peter 3:9). And Jesus says, "I shall draw *all* people to myself" (John 12:32). If God is prepared to break down the barriers that divide us, shouldn't we try to do the same?

Noted American evangelist Tony Campolo tells of visiting an all-night diner in Hawaii while suffering from jet lag and being unable to sleep. From his booth, he overheard a conversation among several "ladies of the night." One said that the next day would be her thirty-ninth birthday, and, sadly, she confessed that she had never in her life had a birthday party. Tony secretly arranged with the manager of the diner to throw a surprise party for the woman. The next night, the woman and her friends were stunned and thrilled, and Tony led the group in prayer.

Later, the diner manager asked Tony, "What kind of church do you belong to?" He replied, "I belong to the kind of church that throws birthday parties for whores at three-thirty in the morning." This was Jesus' kind of church.

CHAPTER   NINE

Reaching Out

It is not always easy to maintain religious faith when we are faced with tragedy or disappointment. Sometimes we are tempted to blame God or feel that we have been abandoned. Human nature apparently requires that we rationalize and concoct defenses, avoiding responsibility even when our mistakes and failures lead to suffering. We tend to feel that God should understand our secret motivations, our general good intentions, and the special circumstances that caused a problem. It is difficult to believe that tribulations are inevitable in life, much less that they can be used as an opportunity to grow.

In his epistle, James teaches us how to deal with the trials of life, including matters over which we have no control. It may be a limitation of talents and abilities that prevents our reaching cherished goals; it may be the loss of a loved one, or the necessity of facing our own deaths. And James says, surprisingly, that we are to face such trials with joy!

My sister Ruth was a successful author and an evangelist who inspired large audiences and ministered personally to countless troubled people. Even now, as I travel the world a decade after her death, people approach me to say, "Your sister Ruth changed my life."

Her faith was beautiful in every way. She loved people and devoted her ministry primarily to those who had lost hope in life. No matter what had happened to them, whether it was drug addiction, alcoholism, infidelity, or crime, she was able to convince them to place the affliction on the shoulders of Christ and in that way to overcome it. She persuaded people that, through simple faith, they could find a way to use their tribulations for the glory of God.

Ruth used a few verses from James as one of the foundations for her ministry: "Consider it pure joy, my brothers, whenever you face trials of many kinds, because you know that the testing of your faith develops perseverance. Perseverance must finish its work so that you may be mature and complete, not lacking anything. Blessed are those who persevere under trial, because when they have stood the test, they will receive the crown of life that God has promised to those who love him" (James 1:2–4, 12).

James' statement is almost impossible to believe, but I reluctantly have come to accept it as true. At one of the most difficult times in my life, Ruth shared her faith with me in a way I'll never forget. Up until 1966, I had been successful in reaching almost all my goals. But that year, after much prayer and soul-searching, I ran for governor of Georgia. When the returns came in, I had lost to Lester Maddox, an avowed segregationist, whose symbol was a pick handle that he used to drive potential black customers from the door of his restaurant in Atlanta. I could not believe that God would let this person beat me and become the governor of our state.

Afterward, I was not only very disappointed with the election but disillusioned about my religious faith. Ruth drove to Plains from her home in North Carolina and asked me to take a walk with her. We sat under a pine tree, and Ruth listened patiently while I bemoaned my misfortune, deplored the poor judgment and racist tendencies of my fellow Georgians, and vented my anger toward God. Then Ruth quoted the second verse of James, that the trials of life should be accepted with joy.

I said, "Ruth, my political life is over! It's not my goal in life just to grow peanuts, sell fertilizer, gin cotton, and build up a bank account. I have nowhere to go! God has rejected me through the people's vote."

Ruth replied, "Jimmy, you have to believe that out of this defeat can come a greater life."

I responded with bitterness, "Ruth, you and I both know that this is nonsense. There is no way I can build on such an embarrassing defeat."

Patiently, Ruth explained what James was saying. When we face trials with courage, we learn to endure and to pray for wisdom. Wisdom can lead us to put our dependence on things that don't change. Lives end, and our health, friends, careers, and financial status all change. We must cling instead to the things we can't buy, things that we can't count or measure but that are available to all through God's love. With faith, we can make the right choices—measured not by our peers or by societal standards but by unchanging priorities. In adversity, Christ can give us enough courage to take a chance on something new. We are not to be discouraged or selfish, not to exclude opportunities for adventure and excitement but to live constantly expanding lives.

If we take a Christian point of view, Ruth concluded, what seems tragic or fearful fades into relative insignificance. The permanent things that characterize the life of Christ become paramount.

Ruth advised me to do something extraordinary, something totally unrelated to my business or politics. I didn't know what this might be, but shortly afterward I was asked by the Baptist Brotherhood to go as a lay witness on a pioneer mission in Pennsylvania. I did, and it changed my religious life forever. But first, what does it mean to be a witness? What is a mission?

One of the most difficult assignments Jesus gave to me and other Christians is to be personal witnesses for our faith. The last command given to followers of Christ during his earthly ministry is clear and unmistakable: "Therefore go and make disciples of all nations. . . . And surely I am with you always, to the very end of the age" (Matthew 28:19, 20). Also in the Book of Acts: "But you

will receive power when the Holy Spirit comes on you; and
you will be my witnesses in Jerusalem, and in all Judea and
Samaria, and to the ends of the earth" (Acts 1:8).

Even as a young boy, I had this mandate ingrained in me
as a personal responsibility. Later I shared with other
church members the duty of visiting every local family
known to us who were not actively worshiping in one of the
neighborhood churches. This task was especially emphasized just before our annual summer revival, when the
pastor and members of our brotherhood would ensure that
all "unchurched" citizens in the Plains community were
invited to attend the worship services. During our sessions
with each family, usually in their front parlors, we would
often explain the plan of salvation, but our primary goal
was to have them join us for the services. We expected the
evangelistic sermons of our visiting preacher to bring the
"lost" to faith in Jesus Christ.

Another man and I were often assigned the names of
some of my own farmer customers. To confront my friends
in this way was embarrassing, but during revival times our
congregation was permeated with a spirit of prayer, fellowship, and mutual commitment, and we never failed to perform our duty. A number of the visits would prove
successful, resulting in new attendees at our services, but
some people I visited each year always rejected our efforts.
Yet even this group seemed to welcome our visits. A few
really liked to debate the biblical issues and were as well
versed in the Scriptures as we. One of their predictable
arguments was to name some of the members of our
church whom they considered sinful. One older man

always maintained that he was not worthy to enter a place of worship because of previous unnamed transgressions for which God, he believed, had never forgiven him. However, he did permit all his children to join the church, and both of his sons later became deacons.

Although the old-fashioned revival fervor is missing today in Plains, the members of our church, particularly we deacons, habitually comply with the command of Jesus by joining the pastor in visiting newcomers to our community to welcome them and invite them to join us at church.

Reaching out to others in an effort to help them understand the liberating message of Christ—that is, witnessing to Christ—is one of several ways that we Christians practice our faith. The degree of emphasis we place on each of these ways often causes debate or dissension among us.

One of these paths is a life of contemplation, based on prayer and regular communion with God. Monastic life is the classic example of this way of serving Christ. This can be very beneficial if used to search for more effective ways to strengthen and to demonstrate our faith. However, as James said, "Faith without works is dead" (James 2:26). Therefore, the contemplative Christian must be careful not to fall into a life devoid of service to others.

Another way of Christian living is to emphasize the avoidance of sin, striving for a virtuous or holy existence. Again, this is a worthy goal, but one that can lead to isolation from others, a highly subjective definition of what is sinful, and a sense of superiority. A person who chooses this path must live and work in close fellowship with others, so as not to become self-absorbed or judgmental.

The third path is to seek to be filled with the Holy Spirit, often called a charismatic life, sometimes exemplified by speaking in tongues. My sister Ruth had experiences of this kind, and I envied her for the intensity and powerful emotion of her spiritual life. There is a clear scriptural basis for this way of Christian living. Paul said that he spoke in tongues more than others, but he also reminded us that it is fruitless if we speak in tongues that have no relation or benefit to others (1 Corinthians 14:6).

Some Christians choose to emphasize compassion for others and a striving for social justice. Christians and others of faith have done much good in the world as a result of their commitment to service. However, service can become just another social program, or one designed to exalt ourselves. Jesus warns that we should perform acts of kindness secretly and always in the name of God rather than as a way of drawing attention or praise to ourselves. As do the other Christian paths, this one offers both opportunities and dangers.

Another way of Christian life is to witness through preaching about Christ. There are some dedicated and inspirational Christian leaders who speak with conviction and effectiveness. For many years, Billy Graham has been justifiably the most admired man in America. He reaches millions with his sermons, and his personal life is looked upon as compatible with what he preaches.

All of these can be effective ways of serving Christ. The problem comes when a Christian assumes one or two of

these roles, emphasizes them as most important, and dero-
gates the others. I, for instance, look on the more inner-
directed ways of Christian life, such as the contemplative
path, as less important than active witnessing by serving
the poor and needy. This is why I derive so much satisfaction from The Carter Center's work in Africa or helping to
build homes through Habitat for Humanity. Some major
churches, in my opinion, overemphasize the importance of
preaching as a means to increase membership and fail to
reach out with compassion to their own neighbors in need.

The fact is that every Christian should attempt to adopt
a strong element of all five ways to practice our faith, and
not judge others who worship Christ differently. The
important thing is that we take our Christian faith seriously
and consider thoughtfully how best to express it in our
lives.

Most of us Christians have a relationship with Christ
that is fairly casual. The presence of the Holy Spirit in our
lives is not total. I'm often filled with doubt; I lack courage,
determination, commitment, and certainty. Yet I'd like to
mold my life and my relationships to be more compatible
with the examples set for us by Jesus and the early disciples
who made a total commitment to their faith under the
most difficult of circumstances.

Jesus, John the Baptist, and the Old Testament prophets
all condemned those who publicly professed their faith,
assumed a devout demeanor, and then betrayed the divine
covenant they claimed to honor. This was a betrayal not
only of God but of themselves.

A lukewarm faith is easy to practice but worth little.

Jesus spoke of it in surprisingly harsh terms: "I know your works; you are neither cold nor hot. I wish that you were either cold or hot. So, because you are lukewarm, and neither cold nor hot, I am about to spit you out of my mouth" (Revelation 3:15, 16). To me, these are some of the most disturbing words he ever spoke. They made little impression on me, a fairly proud and self-satisfied Christian, until one morning when our pastor at Plains Baptist Church preached a sermon with the title "If You Were Arrested for Being a Christian, Would There Be Enough Evidence to Convict You?"

I began to think about the questions the prosecutors might ask me: "What have you actually done for others in the name of Christ?" "Have you ever made sacrificial gifts of time or money?" "How many of the very poor families in Plains do you really know?" "Have you visited them in their homes?" "If you are not a Christian, why are you a member of the church?"

Defending myself against the charge of being a Christian wouldn't be hard. I could imagine explaining with great conviction that, except during the Thanksgiving and Christmas seasons, I had rarely associated with the really poor citizens of our community. I knew those who were my customers and employed a few of them to shovel peanuts, load fertilizer, or drive my trucks and tractors, but these relationships were strictly business. No evidence could be presented that I associated with them socially, and I certainly had never sacrificed the interests of my own family for the benefit of these people.

As far as my church membership was concerned, there

were obvious social and financial advantages in being part of the largest and most influential congregation in town. Many of my potential customers for insurance, fertilizer, seed, and other farm supplies were my fellow Baptists, and a non-Christian businessman would be almost an outcast in our small community. The pastor of our church was a sincere speaker who entertained us every week and made us feel contented with ourselves because we attended his services. Also, my family and I enjoyed our fellowship with other church members and the social events sponsored by the church.

I could admit that, as a good citizen, I obeyed the laws of my state and nation. But was I guilty of walking an extra mile? Turning the other cheek? Loving my enemies? Making gifts in secret? Rarely, or never! I certainly was not one of the extremists who tried to conform my life to the radical elements of the Sermon on the Mount.

All in all, there was little evidence that I was anything other than a lukewarm follower of Christ.

For many of us Christians, one of the old stories about St. Peter is applicable. A man approached the gates of heaven and was asked for his credentials. "Well," he said, "during the Depression years I saw a starving family on the street and gave them fifty cents. More recently, my neighbors' house burned down, and I gave them a table that cost me a half dollar." An angel checked the record and found the two reports accurate. The angel then asked what should be done, and St. Peter replied, "Give him his dollar back and tell him to go to hell."

We tend to define religion, Christ, and Christianity in

the most convenient way. It's much easier to discuss doctrine and the nuances of theology than to read and follow Jesus' words in the New Testament. C. S. Lewis suggested that our own devised religions inevitably stand in the way of our growth into true Christians. If our religion identifies God just with our own peace of mind and our social and economic welfare, our religious lives will be narrow and shallow, instead of broad and deep.

Some leaders of congregations tend to regard church attendance as a sufficient service to God and as an adequate repayment for his blessings. Reaching out to others in the name of Christ is of great importance only if it is not a superficial act. What is significant is the permanent impact on a person's way of living, continuing growth in relation to God—not just the name on a church roll.

Some of our most famous Protestant churches are growing by leaps and bounds, making membership so appealing to earthly ambitions that their pastors are almost exalted as little saviors. The implied message is, "Just look at the advantages of Christian fellowship. If you are an insurance salesman and you join our church, we've got 1,500 members who might need insurance. It's a natural thing, you know, to do business with a fellow worshiper."

We have seen the trend for some preeminent downtown congregations to sell their property in the increasingly troubled city neighborhoods and move into the suburbs, which have a more affluent and homogeneous population. Some spend millions of dollars installing recreation facilities that compete with the finest country clubs.

The "Doonesbury" comic strip once had a series about

some yuppies who were looking for a church to attend. They went from one church to another, and they rejected the ones that emphasized atonement for sin or the need to change the way they lived. "Oh, we can't accept that," they said. They went to another church that had a ministry in the inner-city neighborhoods, which would have required some of their time. No, they didn't want that. They finally chose a large and beautiful church—because it had a racquetball court. As Cecil Sherman, leader of the Cooperative Baptist Fellowship, would say, "This church was majoring in the minors."

When I was campaigning for president in 1976, I visited one of the most famous television evangelists. We drove through a large, ornate gate, with uniformed guards on duty, up a circuitous driveway through a beautifully land-scaped woodland and garden area, and arrived in front of an ornate mansion—his home. When I politely mentioned the seclusion and luxury of the place, he replied that he needed some privacy from his many admirers, and that the entire estate had been "dedicated to the Lord." He and his family were just using it during their lifetimes. Strangely, I didn't feel that I was in the presence of Jesus.

A *living* Christian faith is both demanding and rewarding. My most memorable religious experiences have been when I reached out to others in personal witnessing efforts and in our annual Habitat for Humanity work projects. The common thread is the clear religious atmosphere, the opportunity for binding with others who are different,

a deep and difficult challenge, a sense of selflessness, and
the faith that our best efforts will be rewarded with success.
Fundamentally, however, these euphoric moments have
grown out of simple but meaningful acts of giving and
sharing. The first of these was the pioneer mission I served
on in Pennsylvania in 1967, following my electoral defeat
and my pivotal conversation with Ruth.

With a small budget and a WATS line that could be
used only at night and on weekends, a group of volunteers
at Pennsylvania State University had called everyone in the
telephone book of Lock Haven, a nearby city. Their purpose was to identify those who had no religious faith and
would accept a visitor to discuss the subject. About a hundred were found, and my task was to visit these families and
talk to them about my faith. My partner was a farmer from
Texas named Milo Pennington, who had been on other
missions of this kind. This was a new experience for me,
and I was both nervous and somewhat embarrassed, but
when I met Milo he tried to reassure me: "We don't have
to worry about the reception we will get or the results of
our efforts. We'll pray a lot, do our best, and depend on the
presence of the Holy Spirit to determine the outcome."
This attitude was foreign to me as someone with a strong
sense of personal responsibility, usually determined to
accomplish every task I set out to do. The idea of letting
God have the responsibility puzzled me, and my nervous-
ness was only partially alleviated.

Nevertheless, Milo and I found a three-dollar-a-day
double room at the YMCA in Lock Haven, met a state
game and fish ranger who was a Christian and would be our

host and adviser, and embarked on our adventure in this strange city. Following addresses on a handful of three-by-five cards, we went from one home to another and offered a prayer before knocking on each door. With rare exceptions, after we explained our mission, we were invited in to meet with the family members.

Milo was tall and thin, and a simple, relatively uneducated man. I eagerly accepted his offer to do the primary witnessing, and he explained, in very basic terms, the plan of salvation: All of us fall short of the glory or perfection of God, and all deserve punishment. But God loves us, and through his grace, not because we have earned it, he offers us complete forgiveness. Jesus has taken on our punishment, and through repenting and accepting this forgiveness we are reconciled with God and can now have eternal life, with the Holy Spirit dwelling within us.

We found a surprising degree of welcome among the families we visited. Some said they were already Christians, others seemed amused, and still others seemed to have been eagerly awaiting our message and invitation. I admit I was uncomfortable with the fumbling way that Milo made his presentation. He would use simple examples from the lives of workers on his own farm and would tell about his own religious experiences. I was amazed, therefore, at the emotional response of many of the people we visited. We would join them in prayer, often in tears, as they pledged to change their lives and to accept the faith we offered them. I knew that the Holy Spirit was in the room.

One night that week, I called Rosalynn and described some of these extraordinary visits. I told her that I had no trepidation about our future encounters and, strangely, no sense of responsibility for the results of our fumbling presentations. I added, "I feel as if our lives are in the hands of God." This was the first time I'd ever been able to put myself totally in God's power, becoming completely free and letting the Spirit of God take over. And the results we achieved—the transforming experiences we shared with the people we visited—were my first encounter with the miraculous power of Christian faith.

Some of our efforts failed. Once we climbed some outside stairs to see a woman living in a small apartment. When we spoke about how all people fall short of the glory of God, she jumped up from her chair and shouted, "Not me! I don't transgress against God, and I certainly do not deserve any punishment." Despite our further efforts to explain, she ordered us out of her home.

Another memorable visit came later that week, in the poorest part of the city. When we asked a Salvation Army worker how to find our targeted address, she told us it was above some stores and then asked if we *really* wanted to go there.

As we entered an alley door, we heard a stream of invective coming from above—language I'd heard only a few times while in the navy—but this time it was in a female voice. Milo and I looked at each other and finally decided to continue. The woman received us with amusement and soon let us know that she was the madam of a small whorehouse, with three other "girls" working with her.

She obviously enjoyed arguing with us and asking leading questions, which we answered as effectively as possible. Eventually, we began to talk about her background and found her to be especially bitter toward her parents, on whom she blamed her present plight. Her father, she said, had made improper sexual advances toward her. As a teenager, she finally had the nerve to tell her mother. An angry and tearful family confrontation resulted, and both parents accused her of lying and being obsessed with sexual fantasies. She ran away from home and began her life as a prostitute "to support myself," she said. She had had no contact with her family for eight years.

We had been there almost two hours, when she said we would have to leave, but she invited us to come back the next day—our last in Lock Haven. We prayed for guidance that night, but our return brought no miracles. We read in John 8:2–11, where Jesus forgives the woman "taken in adultery" and says to her accusers and would-be executioners, "Let him that is without sin among you cast the first stone." He then tells the woman, "I do not condemn you. Go, and sin no more."

Despite our best efforts, this woman could not consider herself worthy of God's forgiveness—because at that time she was not willing to "sin no more." She did agree to call her parents, though, and actually dialed their number while we were there. When there was no answer, she promised to try again later. I have prayed often that she was reconciled with God and her parents.

Despite these apparent failures, more than forty people in Lock Haven agreed to start a new church, and we helped them rent an abandoned building near the end of the runway of Piper Aircraft Company. I came home from

Pennsylvania with a heightened sense of the intimacy possible between a human being and God.

The next year I went on a missionary trip to Springfield, Massachusetts, with five other men from Georgia. This was a real adventure for members of the Plains church, not only to go to a strange and somewhat foreboding new community but to test our knowledge of the Scriptures. My assignment was to witness to Spanish-speaking families, most of whom were from Puerto Rico. They were very poor and lived in ramshackle, almost abandoned apartment buildings near a large textile mill that had closed. Those who were lucky enough to find work would travel in buses to labor in nearby fields of vegetables and shade-grown tobacco.

We stayed in a YMCA and would go each day from one large building to another, visiting the families crowded together in it. My partner was a remarkable Cuban-American named Eloy Cruz, the pastor of a small church in Brooklyn, New York. I was quite proud when I was chosen for this task because I knew a foreign language. However, Reverend Cruz and I soon realized that the Spanish vocabulary I had known and used in the navy was quite different from the one we were now using to teach the Gospel!

Reverend Cruz did almost all the witnessing; my contribution was limited to reading the Bible verses that we chose in advance of each visit. I was amazed at how effective Reverend Cruz was in reaching people's hearts. They would become quite emotional when he explained to them some aspect of Jesus' ministry and how his life could relate to them.

Once a woman opened her door surrounded by five or six children. When we told them the reason for our visit, her husband, who was sitting across the cluttered room, immediately tried to hide a half-empty beer bottle behind his chair. As Eloy Cruz explained the story, I read from the Book of John about Lazarus, Mary, and Martha, three of Jesus' closest friends. Lazarus had died, and Jesus was preparing to restore him to life. This was a dramatic story, even with my inept reading of the Spanish Scripture. After Jesus wept, and then called to Lazarus, our listeners waited breathlessly. When the dead man came forth from the tomb, everyone broke into cheers. Later, they knelt with Reverend Cruz and me and accepted Christ as Savior.

I had wonderful experiences every day as I worked with this remarkable man. He always seemed to know exactly what to say and seemed to form an instant intimacy with the people whose homes we entered. With the simplest words, he could capture their imaginations and souls. I was as overwhelmed as they and several times had tears running down my cheeks.

I was embarrassed by the deference with which Eloy Cruz treated me. For one thing, I owned an automobile—something he'd never dreamed of having. Furthermore, I had been a state senator and even a candidate for governor (he seemed to ignore my defeat!). He considered himself "just" a Cuban, and a refugee, but I knew the opposite: He was a great man.

As we prepared to say good-bye at the end of the week, I asked him about what made him so gentle but so effective as a Christian witness, and he was quite disconcerted. He finally said, *"Pues, Nuestro Señor no puede hacer mucho con un hombre que es duro."* (Well, our Savior cannot do much with a man who is hard.) He noted that Christ himself, although the Son of God, was always gentle, especially with those who were poor or weak. He went on to say that he always tried to follow a simple rule: "You only have to have two loves in your life—for God, and for the person in front of you at any particular time."

Eloy Cruz's words express a profound and challenging theology. It requires courage and a lot of humility, because there has to be a sense of equality when you love someone else. To put myself on an equal basis with a homeless person, a drug addict, or someone who might be lonely or in need tends to make me feel uncomfortable. In fact, when I do this, I am ennobling them—and myself. This is not just an idealistic theory, because I know from a few such occasions in my life that it is true.

After these home mission experiences, when I was preparing to run for governor a second time, I was invited to speak to the men's brotherhood in a nearby church about my experiences as a Christian witness. I went to my front room to write my speech, very proud that they had recognized my performance in personal evangelism. I began to write down my achievements. I computed that in all my visits, in Pennsylvania, Massachusetts, Atlanta, and around my own community, I had witnessed successfully to 140 people.

I wrote down the figure, but I guess the Lord must have been looking over my shoulder, because I immediately remembered the frantic 1966 political campaign, when Rosalynn and I had gone throughout the state and shaken hands with 300,000 Georgians, extolled my good points, and asked them to support me for governor. The difference between the hundreds of thousands of personal visits on my own behalf in a few weeks and the small number over a lifetime for Christ was a reminder of how little I had done compared with the potential of my religious life.

But although my activities as a Christian witness have been relatively modest, they have given me both experiences of the power of the Holy Spirit that have shaped my life as a Christian and memories I'll never forget.

CHAPTER TEN

The Lord I've Come to Know

People in my Sunday school classes like to ask questions about religion and my own beliefs concerning God, Jesus, the Holy Spirit, and the church. There are a few extensively marked religious books in my library, and it has been useful for me to learn from them how some Christian theologians define religion.

Karl Barth said that religion is our search for God, and that this always results in our finding a god that is most convenient for our own purposes. He distinguishes this from faith, which results from God's seeking us through Christ.

Dietrich Bonhoeffer saw religion as "dividing life and

the world into two spheres, sacred and secular, or holy and profane."

Reinhold Niebuhr maintained that religion is the final battleground between God and man's pride. He also called it "a search for all of life's highest values."

Paul Tillich explained that through religion we seek our proper relation to the ultimate and to other humans. He insisted that we cannot receive answers to questions we do not ask. He said it is all right to be doubtful. "Doubt is not the opposite of faith; it is one element of faith."

Martin Luther said, "Men are not made religious by performing certain actions which are externally good, but they must first have righteous principles, and then they will not fail to perform virtuous actions."

What is meaningful to me is the application of religious ideas to life.

When I was young, my understanding of God was simple and naïve. There were times when I felt confident that all the biblical teachings were absolutely accurate messages to me, inspired by God and surviving almost verbatim in their original form. I knew that the original texts were written mostly in Hebrew and Greek, but I assumed that somehow the scholars who produced the King James Version of the Bible in 1611 were inspired to translate each thought into English with precise accuracy. I believed the legend that the forty-seven men chosen by the British monarch worked independently for several years and then found to their amazement that every word in each of their final texts was exactly the same as in the other forty-six.

At least I wasn't as certain in my beliefs as Miriam "Ma" Ferguson, who was elected governor of Texas in 1924, the year I was born. There was then, as now, an intense debate about whether Spanish should be used in the public schools by children who had recently moved to our country from Mexico. Governor Ferguson, who opposed the use of Spanish, concluded the argument by holding up a Holy Bible and saying, "If English was good enough for Jesus Christ, it's good enough for Texans!"

Except during my childhood, when I was probably influenced by Michelangelo's Sistine Chapel depiction of God with a flowing white beard, I have never tried to project the Creator in any kind of human likeness. The vociferous debates about whether God is male or female seem ridiculous to me. I think of God as an omnipotent and omniscient presence, a spirit that permeates the universe, the essence of truth, nature, being, and life. To me, these are profound and indescribable concepts that seem to be trivialized when expressed in words.

At the same time, I feel a need for a personal relationship and an ability to communicate with God. As a Christian, I have additional knowledge about God from New Testament Scripture: "God is love" (1 John 4:8) and what Jesus told his questioning disciples: "If you have seen me, you have seen the Father" (Luke 14:9). It seems fruitless for me to go any further in trying to analyze the exact character of God.

* * *

My Sunday school students sometimes want to know about the Jesus Seminar, a group of liberal academics who meet annually in their search for "the historical Jesus." It seems that they consider any biblical statement about Jesus fallacious if they can't prove it to their own satisfaction based on the examination of existing records, computer analysis of the Gospel texts, group assessment of the psychological pressures on and attitudes of the disciples, and some fragments of the Dead Sea Scrolls and other ancient scripts. Their stated purpose is to discover the "real" Jesus.

Some of the more radical of the group claim that Paul, Peter, John, Matthew, and others had visions of a risen Christ after his death, perhaps based on guilt about abandoning Jesus or self-hypnosis caused by their urgent psychological need to see a resurrected Savior. One of these scholars' many books states that the more than 500 believers described by Paul were caught up in a "mass ecstasy" that caused them to see Jesus in a vision like those caused by LSD. A scholar from Chicago, John Dominic Crossan, writes that Jesus' body, after having been removed from the cross and left in a sealed tomb, did not rise from the dead but was eaten by wild dogs. An Australian author, Barbara Thiering, claims that Jesus was buried by mistake in a cave by the Dead Sea, not dead but just drugged, and later was revived with a purgative, married Mary Magdalene, had three children, was divorced and remarried, and finally died in Rome.

These scholars have "voted" collectively that only one sentence in Mark's Gospel is authentic, that the Book of John should be completely disregarded, and that only a few phrases in the Sermon on the Mount are authentic. They attempt to write their own individual Gospels, claiming to have more knowledge about the events of the time than did those who knew Jesus, including Paul, who began writing only about fifteen years after the crucifixion. Although there is dispute about dates because of the lack of direct evidence, it is thought that Mark wrote his Gospel about twenty years later and that the other Gospels came soon thereafter. The skeptical scholars use these time intervals to cast doubt on the Scriptures, tending to ignore the accuracy of oral history traditions and claiming that memories thirty to fifty years old are bound to be incorrect. Yet, in fact, I can remember vividly some of the acts and words of my father before I left home for the navy more than fifty years ago.

How could the diminished Jesus they describe, a failed prophet who made no notable statements, who did not rise from the dead, have transformed his timid and disloyal disciples into historic giants willing to become martyrs for their faith? Where would there be a basis for today's worldwide church, with 1.5 billion believers, many of whose lives have been deeply affected by their faith? How could Jesus still be alive to me and other Christians, his life a perfect model for admiration and emulation? How could so many hearts be touched and minds stimulated by Jesus to seek ultimate truths about life? If these naysayers are right and either the Gospel writers and Paul were all liars or their words were largely subverted by later revisionists, then what is the basis for the Christian faith?

Like most other Christians, I read and study the historical evidence about Jesus from archaeology, textual analyses, and sociological and anthropological studies of the Palestine of 2,000 years ago. But when the theories conflict with my basic beliefs and my living experience of Christ, I prefer to rely on faith, confident that further discoveries of ancient texts and other evidence will never disprove what I believe that makes the impact of Jesus on my own life so profound. After all, it is the role of Jesus in reshaping the lives of believers today that matters most.

A crucial stage in the growth of my faith came when I began to see that the teachings of Christ could be applied to a secular existence. Previously, I'd focused my daily activities on ambitions as a naval officer and then as a young, aspiring farmer and businessman: to excel on my ship, to develop the best seed peanuts in the world, to run a successful warehouse and cotton gin, to move into a nice home of our own, to raise a close and happy family, to win public office, and so on. All of these goals I achieved.

The first real defeat in my life had come in 1966, when I lost the governor's race to a racist opponent. As I've already explained, I felt that God had let me down. After all, I thought, I've done a pretty good job of being a Christian! Don't I deserve a better reward than this?

Religious faith helped me turn adversity into opportunities to work as a lay missionary with Milo Pennington

and Eloy Cruz, my first exposures to the miraculous qualities of Christianity. But it also brought home to me in a
stronger way than ever before the disparity between my
secular ambitions and the example of Jesus Christ.

When I turned to the Gospels, the Jesus I met had a very
different way of life from the one I was building for myself
and my family. Jesus had no money, no possessions, no
house; he turned away from his mother, brothers, and sisters; he was abandoned in time of trouble by his friends and
followers; and he died when he was still a young man. How
could this be my God?

I began to realize that when I envisioned a supreme
being, he was more like Muhammad, the founder of Islam,
a patently successful man in earthly terms: a powerful
warrior, political leader, founder of a great institutional
church. This was in many ways the opposite of the Jesus of
the Gospels, or the image of the "suffering servant" in
Isaiah, whom Christians identify with Christ: physically
unattractive, uneloquent, scorned, rejected. The more I
thought about the discrepancy between my image of God
and the image in the Gospels, the more it tortured me, not
for Jesus' sake but for mine—because I was so different
from the divine human being I claimed to worship.

Jesus' rejection of earthly standards of success was a
deliberate and essential aspect of his ministry. There is a
remarkable description in the fourth chapter of the Gospel
of Matthew of how Jesus was severely tempted by the devil
just as he was commencing his earthly ministry. Jesus was
not tempted to do something morally wrong; rather he was
offered easy ways to achieve his own worthy goals.

The first temptation offered to Jesus, who had been fasting for forty days, was a seemingly innocent one: "If you are the Son of God, tell these stones to become bread." Every Jew knew the story of Moses and the Israelites in the desert, to whom manna was delivered each day—as a boy, I thought of this miraculous food as similar to Southern grits. One of the things expected of the promised Messiah was that he would at least have the powers that Moses had. How nice it would be for the nation of Israel if they didn't have to work for their supper anymore!

So this temptation was not illogical or ridiculous, nor was it obviously sinful. It would not only have assuaged Jesus' famished condition after forty days of fasting but also would have demonstrated that he was, indeed, the Messiah. What a quick way this might have been to Christ's ascendance as the supernatural, spiritual leader of the world! It might even have made unnecessary his crucifixion and death.

We can see the attractiveness of this temptation. But if Jesus had succumbed to it, he would have exalted himself and the transient needs of this life at the expense of the eternal. What happened to the Israelites when they got manna from God? Did they stay loyal? No, they took their blessings for granted. And they also came to feel that the alleviation of their human needs was the central point of their belief in God.

After Jesus rejected this temptation, another was offered: "Then the devil took him to the holy city and had him stand on the highest point of the temple. 'If you are the Son of God,' he said, 'throw yourself down, for the scriptures say God's angels will lift you up in their hands, so that you will not strike your foot against a stone.' " It would have been a convincing demonstration of Jesus' divinity if he had stood on top of the temple, leapt into space, stopped his fall just above the ground, walked into the sanctuary, and then preached his sermon! It would have made it much easier for us modern-day Christians to allay our doubts if we could read the Bible and say to ourselves, "If he wasn't the Son of God, how could he fly from the top of the temple?"

Jesus gave a clear and simple reason for rejecting this temptation: "It is written, you shall not tempt the Lord your God" (Matthew 4:7). He made it clear that the Creator's power will not be used for entertainment or to impress believers. Almost all Jesus' miracles were designed to alleviate human grief, loneliness, and physical suffering.

The devil's third and final temptation was his offer to allow Jesus to replace Caesar and other leaders as the ruler of the entire world. Again, the logic of the temptation is powerful. What a wonderful and benevolent government Jesus could have set up! How exemplary the justice would have been! Maybe there would have been Habitat projects all over Israel for anyone who needed a home. And the proud, the rich, and the powerful could not have dominated their fellow citizens.

It is easy to see the attractive nature of this offer. It would have not just exalted Jesus but also set an example for centuries of later rulers. As a twentieth-century governor and president, I would have had a perfect pattern to follow. I could have pointed to the Bible and told other government leaders, "This is what Jesus did 2,000 years ago in government. Why don't we do the same?"

But the devil stipulated fatal provisos: an abandonment of God, and an acknowledgment of earthly things as dominant. Jesus answered, "It is written, 'Worship the Lord your God, and serve only him' " (Matthew 4:10). Anyone who accepts kingship based on serving the devil rather than God will end up a tyrant, not a benevolent leader.

As the story of the temptations in the desert shows, Jesus refused to perform miracles in order to exalt himself or to demonstrate his own greatness. Instead, when he performed extraordinary acts of healing that would have increased his fame and recruited followers, most often he would say, "Don't tell anyone what I have done." There was always a lesson in what Jesus did, sometimes quite subtle, as when he first forgave the sins and only then healed the affliction of the crippled man whose conniving friends lowered him through a roof to gain access to Jesus (Mark 2:2–11). The Pharisees there understood the lesson: Forgiveness and reconciliation with God are more important than being able to walk.

My own attitude toward the miracles of Jesus has gradually changed. At times, they make me uncomfortable; it's not always easy for me to feel complete faith in their validity. But I now believe that, even if some of the more dramatic miracles recounted in the Gospels could be untrue, my faith in him would still be equally precious and unshaken. I am not a Christian because I think that belief in Christ will let me see my father again, or my brother, after I die. That's not a major consideration for me anymore, although it was for a long time. What is important is what Christ means to me as a personal savior, an avenue to God, an example, a guide, and a source of reassurance, strength, and wisdom.

If I could read only one book in the Bible, it would be the Gospel of John. To me, the first few verses, which refer to Jesus as the Word of God, are almost breathtaking, ending with "And the Word was made flesh, and dwelt among us, and we beheld his glory, the glory as of the only begotten of the Father, full of grace and truth" (John 1:14).

One of the most intriguing passages in John describes the relationship between Old Testament beliefs and the revolutionary message of Christ through a series of encounters between Jesus and Nicodemus, a distinguished Jewish leader of his day.

Nicodemus visited Jesus in the first place because of curiosity. He came at night, probably because he didn't want to be seen with Jesus. There was a reason for caution when someone who was, in effect, a member of the Supreme Court and a top law official came to visit a man considered guilty of blasphemy, a crime that could and would be punished by death.

Nicodemus was a devout religious leader who knew and obeyed the Jewish ritual law: how far one could walk on the Sabbath, how to cleanse oneself, what one could eat, how much to give in tithing, and exactly how to perform the religious services. He also knew how to be careful about the kinds of people he touched or even talked with to avoid becoming unclean. All this was delineated in his community's religious rules, and obeying them was an essential aspect of Nicodemus' faith.

However, this night he was willing to ask some troubling questions. Let me summarize his conversation with Jesus:

Nicodemus said, "Because of the miracles you have done, I know that you are a teacher from God."

Jesus replied, "To see God's kingdom, you must be born again."

Nicodemus: "How is it possible for an old man like me to go back into his mother's womb and be born a second time?"

Jesus: "You must be born of water and the spirit, which is like the wind that you can hear and feel but cannot see. How can you be a master of Israel and not understand? We have said what we know and see about earthly things, which you have rejected, so how will you believe heavenly things?"

And then Jesus made a brief statement that describes the foundation for Christianity: "For God so loved the world that he gave his only son, that whoever believes on him will not perish but will have everlasting life. For God sent his son not to condemn the world, but that the world through him might be saved" (John 3:16, 17).

Nicodemus did not grasp what this meant, both because of the strange and mysterious nature of the message and because he was clinging to the way his life had been shaped by his tradition, his family, his wealth, his power, and his privileged status in life. His exact response at that time is not recorded, but we know that he was profoundly affected by these words and continued to search for their meaning.

Later, Nicodemus was to play one of the most dramatic roles in biblical history. When his fellow Pharisees plotted to arrest Jesus, Nicodemus defended him by quoting the law and was even accused by his powerful peers of being a believer in Jesus. The final reference to Nicodemus in the Bible occurs after Jesus' body was removed from the cross, and Joseph of Arimathea had taken it to be buried with the approval of the Roman governor Pontius Pilate: "Nicodemus, who at first had gone to see Jesus at night, went with Joseph, taking with him about one hundred pounds of spices, a mixture of myrrh and aloes. The two men took Jesus' body and wrapped it in linen cloths with the spices, preparing it for burial" (John 19:39–40). Thus, Nicodemus' last appearance is in an act of mercy and generosity.

To emulate the perfect life of Jesus and to comply with his teachings is impossible. God, being perfect, cannot condone sinfulness, and the punishment for our violation of divine laws is separation from God. But through our faith in Christ, who was perfect and who personifies grace and truth, we can be totally forgiven and reconciled with God, for "the gift of God is eternal life through Jesus Christ our Lord" (Romans 6:23).

In my early life, the varied, even paradoxical qualities of Jesus were obstacles to my faith. Only over time, and through the powerful examples of people like Eloy Cruz, Bill Foege, Millard and Linda Fuller, and Jerome and Joann Ethredge, did I begin to comprehend what they meant. I came to realize that the apparent weaknesses of Christ are really what make him precious and give him a quality of authenticity that I now find convincing.

In his last encounter with the disciples before his death, Jesus clearly described his intimate relationship with God, and emphasized his status as the Messiah. It is perhaps the most self-exalting statement he ever made (John 2:44–50). But then he took off his clothes, wrapped himself in a towel, knelt down on the floor, and washed the disciples' feet. This kind of image is profoundly important to me as I try, in my own way, to follow Jesus' example: for instance, when I go with a Habitat team to build a house in Los Angeles or Chicago, inhabited by the poorest Americans, surrounded by drug addicts and criminals, sometimes with gunfire resounding on nearby streets. (One of our Habitat volunteers, a teenager, was actually hit by a pistol shot as we worked on a house in Miami.) The awareness that my God walked this way before me makes it possible to sustain such an effort.

To me personally, Jesus bridges the tremendous chasm between human beings and the seemingly remote and omnipotent God the Creator. The more I learn about Jesus, the more complex and challenging are his teachings, and the more closely connected are God the Father and God the Son. It really comforts and satisfies me to equate the almighty Creator with the humble but perfect Jesus, and to remember that "God is love."

People in my Sunday School class often ask what it

means to be a Christian. My best explanation is that a Christian is a person professing Jesus Christ as a personal savior, and striving to have the qualities demonstrated by Jesus.

God is committed to absolute purity and justice but also filled with grace, forgiveness, and love. For me, the indefinable character of God can be envisioned only through the mixture of these apparently incompatible characteristics in the life of Jesus. He was both God and man, all-powerful, all-knowing, gentle, compassionate, suffering, despised, burdened with the sin of others, abandoned by his followers, publicly executed; but resurrected, and now worshiped by hundreds of millions of believers throughout the world.

God's demand for obedience and an unwillingness to condone sin required some special means for reconciliation between fallible humans and the supreme being. But through God's only son, who was perfect and took the punishment for our sins, we have been given an insight into the nature of God.

True Christianity is a transcendent commitment. It cannot be achieved through our own desire to live right, to be good people, or to share what we have with others. It is not going to church or being baptized. Membership in a church congregation or a religious denomination is not enough. The personal relationship with Christ is the only core around which religious life can exist.

A more private question that I get, usually when a person is leaving my class, is "What can I get from these lessons about Jesus if I am not a Christian?" I explain that personal faith in Christ and a special reverence for him will help to reveal God's transcendent love. However, I have never found anything in the strictly human life of Jesus that was not admirable and inspirational. So whether or not a doubtful person can accept Jesus' divinity, there is in him a model of human existence to be studied and perhaps emulated.

Jesus' intriguing and often delightful experiences are fascinating, and they offer examples of how to deal with our afflictions and concerns in a reassuring and joyful way. They give us priorities or standards for living. Almost any of our most exalted ideals can be explained, clarified, and expanded by what Jesus said and did. Jesus' teachings can help to put us at peace with both our Creator and our neighbors. All of this can be gratifying and valuable, regardless of our public profession of faith.

CHAPTER ELEVEN

Abundant Life

The most unforgettable funeral I've ever attended, maybe with the exception of those of my own family members, was the service for Mrs. Martin Luther King, Sr., mother of our nation's greatest civil rights leader. Her husband, Daddy King, and the whole family were close friends of ours. I and a number of other speakers made brief comments, but there was one truly memorable presentation. Rev. Otis Moss from Cleveland, Ohio, preached a brief but remarkable sermon about "the little dash in between." He said there would be a marker on Mrs. King's grave, with her name and a couple of dates—when she was born and when she died—and a little dash in between. He said he didn't want to talk about when she was born, or when she died, but about that little dash. He described Mrs. King's great life and then shifted his attention to the audience. He said that everybody has what might be considered just a tiny dash but that to us, with God, it is everything. The question is, What do we do with that little dash in between, which represents our life on earth?

Many people my age have cautionary phrases deeply ingrained in us: "A penny saved is a penny earned." "Waste not, want not." "Haste makes waste." During the Great Depression, we were very careful to husband what we had and not be wasteful with what we spent. We learned to live cautiously, to fear debt, and to limit our ambitions and the chances we were willing to take. Most of us still want to be sure we don't give away too much, so we always parcel out a little at a time, making sure we hold back more than we might need.

As a consequence, we often underestimate the gifts we have from God: life, talent, ability, knowledge, freedom, influence, and plenty of opportunities to do something extraordinary. We have to remember that our lives will become shrunken if we act only from a cautious sense of duty. It is the reaching, the inspiration, the extra commitment that provide the foundation for a full and gratifying life.

After we satisfy all our personal needs and desires, then what? It is not through gratifying physical needs that we find our purpose in life. We shouldn't carry around what we are in a closed jar and use a medicine dropper to expend it. The "little dash" can be a glorious experience.

As I go through my years of existence, whether thirty,

fifty, or seventy, what things most occupy my thoughts? What preoccupies me when I'm in my most self-analytical mood?

Is my life meaningful, or at least interesting and gratifying? How do I relate to my spouse, my children, and my grandchildren? Am I happy or at least content with the decisions I am making? Am I taking care of my health? How well do I interact with the people I know? Do I live by the Golden Rule? What kind of reputation or influence will I leave behind? Am I ready for the future, both in this life and after death? Am I helping my community and my nation live up to their ideals?

It's not easy to match these sorts of global thoughts with the mundane experiences of the moment. But there are simple ways to make each day more meaningful. We can't transform the world, but when we are in a grocery line with two or three other people, we can remember our faith or moral values and at least exchange a kind word. As Eloy Cruz said, we can "love God, and the person in front of us."

One common goal in life is happiness, or joy, and it is the keeping of God's commandments that provides us with a real opportunity to experience this joy. The Scriptures say, "If you keep my commandments, you shall abide in my love. . . . These things have I spoken unto you, that my joy might remain in you, and that your joy might be full" (John 15:10, 11).

When was the last time we felt almost totally at ease within ourselves? Through religious faith we are also promised peace, even when we are worried or filled with fear: "My peace I give unto you. . . . Let not your heart be troubled, neither let it be afraid" (John 14:27). And we are promised "The peace of God, which passes all understanding" in our hearts and minds (Philippians 4:7). We are offered these blessings through faith.

For The Carter Center, Rosalynn and I still maintain a full schedule of travel and activities, and we visit regularly with destitute and suffering people in places like Haiti, Ethiopia, Rwanda, Bangladesh, and the ghetto areas of America's cities. It is not often that we spend time with people in an affluent society who seem to be completely at peace *without* television, electricity, automobiles, telephones, and other "necessities."

Recently, though, we went to Indiana and visited with an Amish bishop. Although his farm and home were comfortable and beautiful, the family attempted to continue a special kind of set-aside life, as had their ancestors as far back as the sixteenth century. We were met at the door by two small girls, about four or five years old. We soon learned that they didn't speak English; their language would be restricted to Pennsylvania Dutch until they began their formal school education at the age of six. There were no telephone or electrical lines entering the home, the fields were cultivated by hand and with plows pulled by horses, and black buggies were used for transportation. The large family gathered around us and seemed to be intrigued by our stream of questions.

The Amish religion is based on the New Testament, with an emphasis on Jesus' Sermon on the Mount, and the

Amish do not accept any intermediary between the individual and God. All their religious services are held in private homes, and when a congregation grows too large to
meet comfortably in a house, they split into two groups. A
pastor is chosen by lot from among the men. The bishop
places a marker in one of a group of hymnbooks, and then
each man selects a book. The one who draws the marker is
assumed to have been ordained by God as the new leader.
Bishops, who usually serve from two to four congregations, are chosen in the same manner from among the pastors. They are considered to be servants; they help resolve
any disputes or issues that arise but have very little actual
authority over others.

For each worship service, a big black wagon full of
benches is driven to the designated home, and the worshipers gather. No one knows in advance who will preach
the morning sermon; again, this leader for the day is
chosen by lot or by last-minute consensus. I asked the
bishop how people could prepare for a sermon if they
didn't know when they would be called, and he replied,
with a genuinely modest attitude, "We always have to be
prepared." For Rosalynn and me, it was an interesting and
inspirational visit.

A few months later, there was a story in my Sunday
school lesson text about a group of Christian laymen
involved in missionary work who descended on a small village near an Amish settlement. As is often the habit of
eager amateurs seeking a possible convert, they confronted
an Amish farmer and asked him, "Brother, are you a Christian?" The farmer thought for a moment and then said,

"Wait just a few minutes." He wrote down a list of names on a tablet and handed it to the lay evangelist. "Here is a list of people who know me best. Please ask *them* if I am a Christian."

I can understand why a number of our Mennonite friends left the Amish faith because of their desire for higher education and in order to use their talents in our technological society. However, both the Amish and the Mennonites offer significant examples of Christian living for me because of their apparently successful attempt to live out, within their close-knit families and communities, the principles of peace, humility, and service above the grasping for modern luxuries.

In addition to a life of joy and peace, we want a life that is focused in a meaningful way.

When I was in school, my classmates and I used to sprinkle iron filings on a piece of cardboard or paper and then put a magnet underneath to see the filings concentrate and make interesting designs. As the magnet moves, so do the filings, but they are always focused on a certain point.

What things in life cause our interests to be concentrated or brought into a proper perspective? Or are our interests like a pile of iron filings without a magnet? Many things can serve as worthwhile focal points for our lives. For some people, it may be enough just to take care of their families, the people they love. This can be beautiful and gratifying.

When I was a child, I would visit my grandmother, who was almost exactly the opposite of my flamboyant grandfather. He was hyperactive, often impatient with others, and always searching for a new project to undertake. The last thing he wanted to do was stay around the house, even during his brief periods without a real job. Grandma was calm, sedentary, and perfectly satisfied with her home-centered way of life. She would concentrate on preparing breakfast for a big family, getting the children off to school, cleaning the house, and working in the garden.

She also had to cook a big noon meal, wash and iron the family's clothes, and then prepare supper. By the time it was dark, we'd go to bed. On Sundays, everyone went to Sunday school and church, so Grandma had to prepare the large dinner in advance, perhaps just cooking the biscuits and fried chicken after the services were over. For one afternoon a week, she joined some other ladies in a quilting bee, sewing while they discussed the affairs of their families and the community.

Although her family more or less took her for granted, I can see now that hers was a complete life of service and dedication, focused on other members of her family.

For most of us, a life of such peaceful service seems foreign or inappropriate, especially in the competitive, high-pressure world of today. Many people wonder how to reconcile belief in a loving God with the uncertainty, anxiety, and fear we all feel from time to time over the dangers and difficulties of life.

The twentieth-century theologian Paul Tillich maintained that *anxiety* grows out of the awareness of our own fragility, uncertainty, and impending death. By contrast, *fear* is of a specific, identifiable threat or object that can be faced or endured with courage. Tillich said that we should strive to change overwhelming anxiety into fear, with which we may deal more effectively.

Fear, then, seems to be transient and justified; anxiety seems to be more permanent and about things imagined or unknown. Fear and anxiety are two of the most troubling human emotions. But we can greatly reduce our feelings of worry and despair if we have faith in ourselves. First having faith in God is the best avenue to this goal.

We have to realize that much of our suffering is the result of our own actions. If we commit crimes and have to serve time or pay a fine, that's not God's punishment. If we lead a selfish or egocentric life and end up with few friends, our loneliness is not God's punishment. If someone jumps off the top of a building, we can't expect God to suspend the laws of gravity. Extensive studies at The Carter Center have shown that two-thirds of our physical ailments and premature deaths are caused by our own choice of lifestyle—smoking, improper diet, lack of exercise, sexual promiscuity, carelessness with firearms, and driving while intoxicated. With God's help, these semisuicidal habits can be changed.

There is a general realization that alcoholism and drug addiction are diseases, but by a combination of self-will, faith in God, and support from others, it is possible to correct or cure them. I have seen personal evidence of this in the experiences of my brother, Billy, who became an apparently hopeless alcoholic while I was president. But ten years before his death Billy decided on his own, encouraged by his wife, Sybil, to combat his addiction. He never drank again, was reconciled with his family, and lived a full life. During these years, he and Sybil worked with thousands of others who were struggling to break their dependence on alcohol and drugs.

Of course, we must confront head-on the small but troubling problems that cause us worry and tend to lure us away from the important commitments of our lives. The New Testament tells us to go ahead and struggle with these challenges but to keep clearly before us the simple, pure, comprehensible reassurance that we can draw from the life and teachings of Jesus. In this we have a great reservoir of strength and power to guide us through both the troubling and disappointing times and the exuberant and successful times.

The Bible message is that each of us is blessed with God's love and grace, overcoming fear:

For God has given us a spirit of fear, but also a spirit of power, of love, and of self-confidence. (2 Timothy 1:7)

So we say with confidence, "The Lord is my helper; I will not fear what man can do to me." (Hebrews 13:6)

There is no fear in love, but perfect love casts out fear; for fear has to do with punishment, and whoever fears has not reached perfection in love. (1 John 4:18)

Do not let your hearts be troubled. Believe in God, believe also in me. (John 14:1)

As I grow older, I have a greater daily awareness that death will one day claim me. Sometimes when I watch a beautiful sunset or have a delightful experience with Rosalynn or my grandchildren, I wonder how many more of these I will see. It is sobering to realize that our inevitable fate is physical death, apparent proof of the relative insignificance of our earthly lives. To people who can't accept this fact with equanimity, death becomes an overwhelming tragedy and a source of constant distress.

However, the realization of our mortality and its correlation with our daily lives is one of the challenges that can be met most effectively by our faith. Except for giving us incentive to live a fuller life, knowledge of our coming death should not affect our spiritual or secular attitudes. My own religious faith is strengthened when I seek God's help in facing the inevitability of death and other uncontrollable or unpredictable events.

Ultimately, we have to find the ability to face the uncertainties of life with equanimity, and a commitment to a higher calling is often the best source of strength. Everyone who serves in the military in times of combat must accept the potential danger. As a young submariner, I realized the inherent risks and was willing to face them.

There was even a strange sense of liberation when we left port for a few weeks, with our responsibilities limited to those within the confines of the submarine hull. Monthly reports concerning personnel and equipment were minimal, and even the cherished duties of a husband and father were left behind. I would be with seventy-one other men for a fairly certain time, putting in to a few ports as scheduled. The duties were onerous but—with the exception of unforeseen crises in operation—routine and predictable. The simplicity of this life was surprisingly satisfying. I dealt with potential concerns, even the possibility of tragedy, by focusing on my duties, realizing that all results could not be within my own control, and honoring my task as worthy of the danger involved.

On ship, we all knew that a few dozen men shared a bond, each depending on all the others. I had faith in the abilities and steadfastness of my fellow crewmen. Still, on at least three occasions, I thought that I would likely die. One example is especially memorable.

Our old fleet-type submarine could operate submerged for only a short time, by drawing a limited supply of electric power from batteries, so we spent most of the time on the surface of the sea. Even then, our ship was almost submerged, with only a very low, flat deck along the pressure hull just above the surface. The bridge was about eight feet higher. Once I was on the bridge at night in a storm, as we proceeded slowly with our bow held carefully facing the large waves. Quite frequently, a swell would rise under me, the water washing around my ankles.

Then suddenly an enormous wave lifted me off my feet, tearing my hands loose from the safety rail. For fifteen or twenty seconds, I swam freely in the sea, not knowing where I was. Then the wave receded, planting me on the low deck behind where I had been standing. I was not injured, and I scrambled frantically back up on the bridge before another wave came along. Had the ship been moving at the slightest angle to the surging sea, I would have come down in the water and been lost in the dark.

Although all of us studied, planned, and practiced to minimize danger, we had made a commitment to serve our country, and we accepted the risks with a feeling of inevitability. We felt that our cause was worthy, we wanted our lives to be significant, and we had faith in one another, our ship, and America. There are somewhat similar concepts in my religious beliefs.

If we are people of faith, we should remember the things that are important in the eyes of God, the surpassing concepts that should influence us. Whether we like it or not, longevity is not one of them. If we have faith in God's promises, we face life beyond our earthly years with equanimity, if not anticipation. Jesus has promised to prepare a place for us.

At any time, we can empty ourselves of anxiety and turn to God. But doing so requires a deliberate effort, or at least a willingness to change our focus from transient things to something that will never be lost. This can be found through Christ and his promise: "And I give unto them eternal life; and they shall never perish, neither shall any man pluck them out of my hand" (John 10:28).

Jesus used a simple verse to emphasize that this opportunity for an intimate relationship with him is always available, but we have to respond: "Behold, I stand at the door and knock. If anyone will hear my voice and open the door, I will come in and have supper with him" (Revelation 3:20). For Christians, this intimacy is what shapes our spiritual life. It is a powerful force, a source of joy, or as I mentioned earlier, the "peace that passes understanding" (Philippians 4:7).

I remember how stricken I felt when I learned that my father had a terminal illness. I was far away, in the navy, and though a grown man, I lay across the bed and wept. Later I witnessed the deaths of my mother, both my sisters, and my only brother. In all these cases, we knew that they had terminal cancer and that death was imminent. The finest medical care was available to them, but all four chose to spend their last days without artificial life-support systems.

With a few family members and friends around them, they died peacefully and within an environment of mutual love and support. Each person seemed to retain his or her lifelong character. My sister Ruth remained deeply religious in her final days; my father tried not to show that he was weak or suffering; my mother urged all of us not to worry about her; my sister Gloria discussed the features of Harley-Davidsons with her biker friends; and my brother, Billy, retained his sense of humor. Even during the last hours of his life, he caused all of us to roar with laughter with a final practical joke or two.

We can face death with fear, anguish, self-torment, and unnecessary distress among those around us. Or, through faith in the promises of God, we can confront the inevitable with courage, equanimity, good humor, and peace. Our last few days or months can be spent in a challenging and exhilarating way, seeking to repair relationships and to leave a good or even noble legacy, in an atmosphere of harmony and love.

Despite religious reassurances, there are times when I miss my family very much and wish they could have shared some of my recent experiences. But my memories of them are pleasant, not filled with anguish or pain.

We would all like to have full and abundant lives. For me, there is a direct response to this desire in something Jesus said: "I am come that they might have life, and they might have it more abundantly" (John 10:10). This full life does not depend on natural talent, IQ, social standing, bank account, or on influence. A full life can be based on seemingly trivial things, simple interrelationships.

Sometimes it seems that there are two parts of our lives. One is when we're rushing to get somewhere on time, or can't decide how to deal with a family crisis, or are hard at work on our jobs. Maybe we are even trying to finish a Habitat house by Friday at noon so we can move folks into their new home. At moments like these, it seems that we can't quite get everything done.

But how do we spend our time when we are not striving, pushing and impatient, with too much to do? We tend to ignore this part of our lives as if it were just the gap between important things. But that nondemanding time is when the fullness of life needs to be nurtured. Who decides what is the quality time? We do.

In 1 Corinthians 13, perhaps the most beautiful chapter in the Bible, Paul emphasizes how relatively insignificant are all kinds of human achievements, even the gifts of prophecy, faith, and generosity, when compared with the gentle and humble act of love. That's a lovely thought, much better than having to do something frantic, ambitious, or competitive. What we are offered in God's love is a new life, but one that is described in such simple terms that we usually pass it by.

The grand things we often spend our days striving to achieve fade into relative insignificance in the little dash, the scope of life from birth to death. It's the simple things, the way we spend our waiting time, that can matter most. So while we are waiting for a profound life experience, or retirement, or death, we are using up the days of our lives. In his letter to the Romans, Paul tells them to be diligent but to act with generosity and joy: "He that gives, let him do it with simplicity, he that shows mercy, with cheerfulness, let love be without dissimulation . . . be kindly affectioned one to another . . . rejoicing in hope, patient in tribulation . . . given to hospitality" (Romans 12:8–13). These words are not telling us to waste time but to act beneficially and joyfully, without pride or criticism of others.

We can follow Paul's advice today. We can take a few minutes on a relaxed day and walk down the street to visit one of our neighbors who is not feeling well or is lonesome and say, "I had some cake left over, and I was thinking about you and I brought you some. I wonder if maybe we could have a cup of coffee together?" It would take less than an hour, but it might be the most enjoyable experience of the entire week. That's the kind of simple thing that won't be on the front page of a newspaper or on television. But we have to be somewhat innovative; it's a shame if we can't think of *anything* to do.

In one of Jesus' parables, the master said, "Well done, good servant! Because you have been trustworthy in a very small thing, take charge of ten cities" (Luke 19:17). He also said, "If you then be not able to do that thing which is least, why take thought for the rest?" (Luke 12:26) and "He that is faithful in that which is least is faithful also in much" (Luke 16:10).

In one of my poems about the people of our town of Plains I refer to their "modest, tempered dreams." Most often, our grandiose dreams are transient in nature, so for all practical purposes we live permanently with our modest, tempered ones. This is not necessarily bad.

Sometimes the simplest things in life can become all-important. Recently Rosalynn and I visited a number of formerly homeless men who had just moved into tiny compartments of their own that had been walled off in old railroad boxcars. They acted as though they owned castles! One of them said, "This will be the first time in many years that I've slept where I could take off my shoes and not tie them to my wrist. Now I can wake up in the morning and know that my shoes will not be gone."

After leaving the White House, I wrote my presidential memoir, *Keeping Faith*, which required careful research into the details of my four years in office. As I examined the 6,000 pages of personal diary notes I had written and the voluminous official documents prepared at the time, I was surprised at how faulty a memory I had. I could hardly recall some truly historic events.

But recently my ten-year-old grandson Joshua and I were out on a little two-person fishing boat with an electric motor, and he wanted to be captain of the ship. He was in the front seat with two buttons that are pushed with your foot to make the boat go right and left. Despite our erratic course, every now and then we caught a nice bass. Just me and my grandson. After a long period of silence, Josh looked at me and said, "Papa, this is the life." It won't appear in any history books, but that was a moment I'll never forget.

A few months later, I had an equally important experience. Our smallest grandchildren were with us, a girl and two boys. They all had an opportunity to go to the movie *The Lion King*. But I had mentioned to the children earlier that we would be raising the water level of our pond over the top of the old pier, so we needed to tear it down. When we tried to get the children to see the movie, they didn't want to go. They insisted on helping Rosalynn and me dismantle the old pier. So we went out and waded around in muck about knee-deep all afternoon, laboriously tearing off the boards, one by one, with crowbars and hammers. We all cheered when the job was finished.

The next morning I had a large backhoe coming in that could have squeezed twice, picked up that whole dock, and dropped it on the bank, crumpled into firewood, so we didn't achieve very much in a practical sense. But what I had instead was another unforgettable experience, just spending an entire afternoon with my wife and grandchildren, sweating and bogging down in the mud.

I like two lessons from Jesus' life that encourage us to

see how small acts of sharing can help us reach beyond normal expectations, routine ambitions, and even the usual standards of religion. One was when Jesus sat down in the temple and watched wealthy people throw sizable offerings into the collection plate. Then he saw a poor widow, who gave two coins, worth less than a penny. He called his disciples to him and said, "Truly I tell you, this poor widow has put in more than all those who are contributing to the treasury. For all of them have contributed out of their abundance; but she out of her poverty has put in everything she had, all she had to live on" (Mark 12:43).

The other event, described in chapter 12 of the Gospel of John, was more strange and dramatic. It concerns a visit with Jesus' friends Mary, Martha, and Lazarus just before he went to Jerusalem to face his accusers and his crucifixion. These three seem to have been Jesus' closest personal friends. It may be that, above and beyond the affection between Jesus and any of his disciples, there was a special closeness between Jesus and Mary. We don't know how much he shared with her about what was going to happen to him, the purpose of his life on earth, and his relationship to God. But we do know there were long periods of time when the two sat together, perhaps in front of her little house, and Jesus explained to Mary the nature of his ministry and perhaps the coming tragic events in Jerusalem. Jesus had told his disciples that he was going to die, but they refused to believe it. Apparently, however, Mary knew and believed. She may have been the only one who did.

This family knew that Jesus liked to have a good time. Some of his parables include memorable and funny events, and Jesus enjoyed outwitting those who were hostile to his teaching. He gave answers to questioners that destroyed their arguments, embarrassed his tormentors, and amused and enlightened the spectators. As far as give-and-take is concerned, he could have taken over easily from David Letterman or Jay Leno. He liked to go to parties and have a good time with strange people who invited him into their homes, including disreputable people like tax collectors and infamous sinners. Many of these happy times in Jesus' life were shared with this family.

It's interesting to conjecture that, after Jesus had raised Lazarus from the grave, his three friends pooled their wealth and considered what they could do to repay him for this miracle. Maybe they were waiting for an appropriate time to entertain him and his disciples. In any case, on this particular night, they threw a party for him. During supper, the Bible says, "Martha served, and Lazarus was one of those reclining at the table with him." Then Mary took a pint of perfume, its value equal to a full year's income for the average worker. She poured it on Jesus' feet and wiped them with her hair.

That's a troubling scene to me. It was an abnormal event 2,000 years ago; it would be even more strange today. The setting is intriguing, the waste of money seemingly inappropriate, the intimacy between the woman and the honored guest disturbing. It was an act far beyond the expected—a transcendent act that described Mary's feelings toward Jesus. Her love for him went beyond boundaries.

Is this just a bizarre ancient story about someone who loved Christ so much that she did what she could to honor him? How does this apply to me and my life?

If I had been there, and I had known that this was the Son of God, who was going to die in six days as a sacrifice for me, I hope that, like Mary, I would have done something dramatic to show him my love and gratitude, without considering whether it might be gauche, excessive, or embarrassing.

The Bible describes Mary's act as a "good" one. The Greek word for "good" is usually *agathos*, but the word here is *kalos*, which is best translated "good and lovely." To me, "good and lovely" brings Mary's act down to a human, intimate level. All of us need to look at ourselves, our circumstances, the environment in which we live, and ask: Within my own talent and realm of possibilities, what can I find to do that would be good and lovely? If we are somewhat embarrassed when considering such acts, perhaps ours is a small world.

God's world is very large, a world we should always explore, to comprehend the problems of troubled people who may be hungry for what we could offer. It's like eating peanuts—if we can decide to be adventurous and generous once, it may be hard to stop! And if we are afraid we'll give away all we have, remember Mary, who had a lot left after the ointment was gone. She had the riches of life and the love of her savior, who, at least symbolically, she had anointed for burial. As we expand our lives and do things that are challenging, innovative, and unpredictable, we can know what it means to be filled with joy and the peace that passes understanding.

A few times in life, a "good and lovely" adventure wouldn't hurt.

Acknowledgments

M y original concept of this book was a collection of some of the more interesting Sunday school lessons I have taught, perhaps fifty-two of them to cover a year of weeks. However, after discussions with my publisher, Peter Osnos, it became clear that it would be better to describe how these Bible texts have helped to shape my Christian faith and how these religious beliefs have affected my life.

Adding these personal elements to the text has been a great challenge, made possible with the help of my wife, Rosalynn, and my two editors, Karl Weber and Nessa Rapoport. With probing questions and suggestions, they have also encouraged me to relate my interpretation of Scriptures to some of the most interesting and controversial issues of modern society. The Rev. Dr. James Bell provided helpful editorial comments on Scripture and theology.

I am grateful to these advisers, and to those people mentioned in this book whose actions, based on faith, have been an inspiration to me.